On the 25th of May 19 Kennedy addressed Co believed the United States should set itself 'the goal, before this decade is out, of landing a man on the Moon and returning him safely to the Earth'. Kennedy's vision became known as the 'Moonshot', a bold move into the future without a clear path to follow. Much of the technology required had yet to be invented; Kennedy didn't know *how* they would get to the Moon exactly, just that they could and would do it if they committed fully as a nation.

On the 20th of July 1969 Kennedy's vision became a reality when Neil Armstrong and Buzz Aldrin walked on the lunar surface. The Moonshot had worked.

Back then it took the vast resources of a global superpower to achieve a history-changing feat that would be felt around the world. A half-century later, in our digital era of exponential returns, we no longer need a country or large corporation to initiate massive change. Today there is sufficient technology in the average smartphone to launch a rocket or start a revolution. All it needs is the right mindset, an understanding of how to do business in the digital world, and your commitment to achieving a transformative, life-changing goal...

I dedicate this book to my parents,
Farivar Sanei and Shahrzad Hone.
Thank you for giving me an upbringing that
has enabled me to get to where I am now
— a place that I love so much.

what's your moonshot?

Future-proof yourself and your business in the age of exponential disruption

JOHNSANEI

with **Kirsten Molyneaux**

ABOUT
THE AUTHOR

John Sanei is a trend specialist, business innovation strategist, entrepreneur, speaker and author.

Having developed his progressive approach to business strategy in boardrooms and in front of audiences across the globe, John is known for his talent to simultaneously entertain, deliver critical insights and inspire change. In applying his Forever Profitable methodology, he encourages courageous decision-making from CEOs, ExCo members and small-business owners; decisions that become instrumental in driving and implementing innovation.

A firm believer that having the right internal dialogue is as important as having the right external strategy, John encourages the people he works with to apply a positive mindset before considering what it takes to participate and succeed in a new age of exponential growth and disruption. His client list includes De Beers, Dell, Microsoft, Oracle, Sappi, Siemens, Standard Bank, Thomson Reuters and Tiger Brands, among others.

Published by Mercury
an imprint of Burnet Media

·

Burnet Media is the publisher of Mercury, Two Dogs and Two Pups books
info@burnetmedia.co.za   www.burnetmedia.co.za
PO Box 53557, Kenilworth, 7745,
South Africa

·

First published 2017
3 5 7 9 8 6 4 2

·

Publication © 2017 Burnet Media
Text © 2017 John Sanei
Author portraits © Melissa Hogarth
Other imagery © iStock by Getty Images, Flat Icon

·

This POD edition printed, bound and distributed by Amazon
www.amazon.com

·

ISBN 9781928230472

Set in Chaparral Pro 11.5pt

Burnet Media | MERCURY

CONTENTS

FOREWORD

BY CAL FUSSMAN

Cal Fussman is a New York Times *bestselling author, celebrated writer-at-large for US* Esquire *magazine, and keynote speaker.*

If you're going to climb a mountain – wherever or whatever that mountain may be – my suggestion is to take John Sanei along with you.

And if John is unavailable, take this book.

Your experience will be different if you are with John one way or another. I know this because one morning not long ago I climbed to the top of Lion's Head mountain in Cape Town with him. And I see the world differently because of the experience.

I had come from the United States to South Africa to speak at events for Suits & Sneakers and RISE of the Nation, both designed to enable the entire country to look at education differently. Access to information on the internet could be a game changer for those who'd been left behind due to years of apartheid, poverty and problems in the standard education system. A small group of local entrepreneurs blessed with education and funding were now asking questions about how they could help South Africa rise to its potential by bringing learning to the masses through the web and guiding that growth into the job market. It was a bold attempt at lifting the country by bringing it together.

I guess I was a fitting speaker for the event. Over the last two decades I'd interviewed a lot of people who'd shaken up the world for *Esquire* magazine. Everyone from Muhammad Ali to Mikhail Gorbachev to Vint Cerf, the creator of the internet. And now I was giving talks about how changing your questions can change your life.

What I didn't count on when I arrived in South Africa was how John and his friends would enable *me* to see the world differently.

It was startling when John confronted me with a fact that is included in this book. In three short years, in 2020, estimates are that 50 percent of the workforce in the United States will be freelancing. The way my country does business has been disrupted and soon will be radically different to what it was only a generation ago.

John and a band of South African entrepreneurs were asking huge questions to disrupt the education system in South Africa for the better. The very size of their questions told me the answers could hold amazing possibilities. As he explained how this disruption could improve lives, he made me very conscious of the disruptions going on all around me.

Once back home, I bypassed a traditional cab and booked a ride using my smartphone with a company called Lyft, which competes against Uber (and others) in the United States. As the driver moved down the highway, I noticed he didn't have his foot on the gas pedal. Our car was moving and stopping with the flow of traffic, and if the driver removed his hands from the steering wheel and the car started to veer out of its lane the electronic system made the correction, straightening the car out and setting it in the centre of the proper lane.

I realised that driverless cars were not ten years down the road; they were almost upon us. I wondered what would happen to the millions of people who were currently driving for a living. And then, as I listened to the radio, I wondered if most of the jobs in radio would be lost when all the riders in cars are able to look at a screen in front of them.

The world is going to be a dramatically different place very soon and people are going to need to identify these disruptions and be educated to get the most out of them.

This is where John and this book come in. The end of the old way is not doomsday. It's a climb up a new mountain. And when you think like John thinks, it's a beautiful climb.

Your life and your business will be richer if you can apply John's thinking and advice to all the disruptions going on around you. That's what this book is about. Getting the most out of changing circumstances.

The world is moving too quickly now to sit by and try to cling to what was. Take the journey up with John. You'll see. The view from the top of the mountain is amazing.

Cal Fussman
Los Angeles, March 2017

PROLOGUE

A QUICK GUIDE TO THE BOOK

I was a multimillionaire by the age of twenty-eight. My success was measured by my financial wealth and I was running on fuel-injected ambition; working hard and riding high. By the age of thirty, I had lost it all.

Although it felt like sudden death at the time, if I think about it now the blow happened in slow motion, right in front of my eyes. Too busy hanging on to the initial years of success, I didn't adapt to a shape-shifting business environment. And I didn't adapt because I was not mentally prepared to even comprehend that it was in fact changing. In the rapid-paced, exponentially evolving digital age, this inability to see the wood for the trees is becoming more and more common in business.

I have spent the past ten years of my life climbing back up the hill while doing my best not to fall down again. This book is a personal recount of my journey and the methodologies I've developed as a result of identifying the need to harness my internal dialogue and mindset to keep up with the ever-changing world.

The Synopsis

An estimated 7 billion people are going to be online and connected to free, fast Wi-Fi within the next five to ten years. In the process, the way the world does business – even the very nature of business – is undergoing the most dramatic and fundamental changes we've seen in a century or more. How are you getting ready for this mass market that is going to be available at the click of a button?

In *What's Your Moonshot?* I will prepare you for the future with the goal of making you and your business financially and intellectually sustainable over the long term – what I call Forever Profitable. If you want to thrive rather than survive, you will need the mindset and business tactics to embrace change. The first step is to get your internal strategy right: are you seeing yourself as a victim of the future, or an architect of it? The second step is to decipher which business strategies, trends and innovations are relevant to you in this era of disruption as you start developing and implementing your 'Moonshot' idea.

Chapter 1 outlines my personal story as the textbook case of why businesses fail today if they're not prepared for the future. For success tomorrow we need to learn the lessons of yesterday.

Chapter 2 examines the roles of mindset and internal dialogue in shaping the habits and patterns of thinking that can turn us into a 'victim', hindering both personal and professional success. Only by identifying the different victim types and traits, can we make a conscious choice to progress past the obstacles we create.

Chapter 3 turns to exploring the 'victor' characteristics and how we can steer our inner voice to switch from being hung up on failure and the need to please others to finding opportunities at every turn.

Chapter 4 introduces the Forever Profitable methodology as a way to examine the future of technology, your industry, your consumer and your employee, before shifting your internal business culture, innovating with purpose and turning to gamification tactics for sustainable implementation.

Chapter 5 reviews examples of successful Moonshots from the past and describes why and how to create a Moonshot of your own.

With a victor mindset and a roadmap to future-proofing your business in the face of disruption, your Moonshot is an opportunity to prepare for the future with optimism and courage. Strap in and get ready for the journey towards becoming the new type of billionaire: one who possesses the courage to think bigger, aim higher and make a positive impact on billions of people.

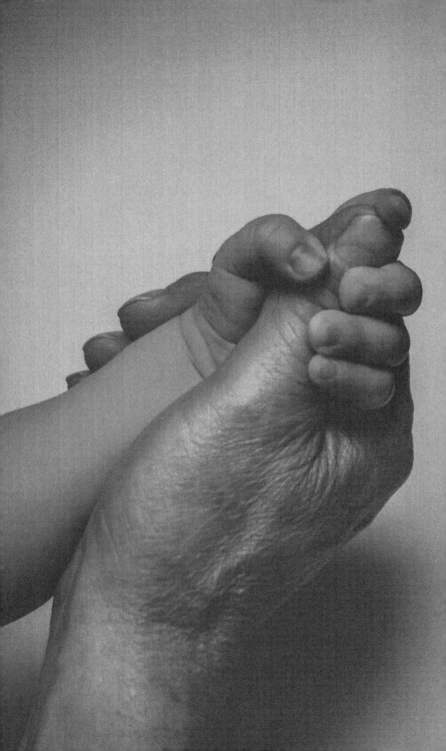

CHAPTER ONE

AGHA-JOON

Learning from past mistakes

My grandfather was my hero. I used to call him *Agha-joon,* an Iranian term of endearment, meaning 'dear man'. He was born in 1900 and passed away at the wise age of 104. He was a wonderful human being and treated me like the apple of his eye – he treated all of his grandchildren in this way.

Agha-joon earned great wealth during his life and yet when he died he was a relatively poor man. His wisdom did not translate into sustained financial success. This always perplexed me, and as a younger man I couldn't understand what had gone wrong for him. How had he been so successful and then somehow lost it all?

It was only after I had started, successfully operated and then lost several businesses that I was able to identify the difference between **becoming** profitable and **remaining** profitable.

Agha-joon once told me a story about bread. He told me that from when he was about ten years old the price of bread didn't increase for thirty-five years. He remembered that the price of bread remained the same until about 1945. And that stuck with me. I thought to myself, 'How is this possible?'

Eventually I realised that time just moved slower back then and that life is very different today: now we are experiencing the world at a super-fast pace in a way that we don't quite understand or know how to react to. I also came to the conclusion that running a business becomes harder in the fast lane (in some ways), because things are constantly and rapidly changing. This notion has driven me to explore the challenges of staying afloat, and inspired me to develop my Forever Profitable methodology. (We'll get back to that.)

Like *Agha-joon*, I had made it big and then lost it all. Not only did I lose my wealth, but, more importantly, for a time I lost my ability to be successful.

It took me a long time to discover that without the right mindset, remaining profitable would be a futile battle. So many of us live to chase success, but when we achieve it we fail to realise that success isn't an end point; we can easily forget that it is a continuous process of looking ahead and staying ahead.

Success is not necessarily a single, awe-inspiring victory.

Small, bite-sized victories are just as valuable as the major milestones that you set out to achieve. Today, I call myself a trend and strategy specialist, a business coach, an entrepreneur and a speaker. My enduring commitment to hold on to these titles with confidence is constantly reinforced by small victories that I celebrate along the way.

I had my first taste of success at a very young age. Looking back, my motivation for success was driven by a need for money and status. My parents had a tumultuous relationship. When they separated I was only eight years old; suddenly I had to become the 'man' of the house. During this time, I was always sensitive to the fact that my mother didn't have enough money to make it to the end of the month and, as a result, I was determined to avoid the hardships of a financially challenged environment.

At the age of thirteen I got my first job packing groceries at our local supermarket. They paid me R3.20 an hour. I used to go to school on a Monday and listen to everyone talk about the latest videos they had watched over the weekend, but I could never join in on the excitement because we didn't have enough money to buy a video machine. I started working after school and on weekends, eager to earn money. After saving my first two salaries, I was able to buy a video machine.

My joy was abruptly interrupted when I realised I also needed a video contract to hire the videos – but I had spent all my money on the machine, so I had to work longer hours and save for another month (by which time I was running out of the *chutzpah* for it). Eventually I got the contract, started watching videos and eagerly joined the conversations with my friends. That was my first experience of what it meant to make money and what I was able to achieve with it.

My ambitions to fit into the social norm didn't end there. When all the kids at school started watching M-Net subscription television, my family again could not afford it. I aimed higher this time and at the age of fifteen I started working as a personal fitness trainer. I made decent money and eventually bought the coveted M-Net decoder and subscription. These first encounters with success were all driven by material ambitions, but they gave me a sense of the freedom and power that money presented. It made me feel victorious – and I was completely hooked.

At the age of twenty-one I moved to London and worked as a bar manager. By the time I returned to South Africa three years later, I had saved quite a bit of money and I began my journey as an entrepreneur. I bought several vending machines and started a shoe distribution business, both of which did well. Around this time, I fell in love with a new restaurant that had opened in Cape Town, called Primi Piatti. The concept was a unique mix of industrial style and contemporary Italian food, and I was blown away by its energy. The brand amazed me in so many ways; it was just what the next generation of diners was hungry for. I had always been an early adopter and had the natural ability to sniff out new and powerful ideas. When I experienced the restaurant for the first time I thought to myself, 'This is going to pump!'

Before long, I owned the first of the brand's franchise restaurants in Constantia, Cape Town. It was a magical experience. I sold my vending machines and the shoe business to focus on my restaurant, which became my life and my passion. For the eight years that I was with the brand, I owned (and sold) a total of six franchise restaurants in Cape Town, Johannesburg and Pretoria. I started earning a lot of money and was catapulted into a world in which I held both power and position. This also meant I had to learn how to become a leader and run multiple businesses at the same time. I felt bulletproof, and thought I had everything I had always dreamed of.

After buying my sixth franchise, one of the restaurants started faltering. In hindsight, the area that it was based in was not doing that well any more and the brand had lost some of its original charm. Instead of looking at how I could adjust to the changing times, I used my cash reserves to top up the losses while trying to sell the ailing restaurant. My downhill run had begun.

After eighteen months of cash injections and trying to sell, I ran out of money and I had to declare bankruptcy. One of my restaurants went insolvent and the rest of them folded because they were no longer generating enough profit.

Over the course of two years, I dropped from being a multimillionaire with a portfolio of assets at the age of twenty-eight to a man with nothing. All of it was gone. I lost my fancy wheels and my fancy house and moved into my friend's second bedroom, penniless and car-less.

My early thirties were **rough years for me**; I had **lost my personality** along with my bank balance.

It was the beginning of the realisation that I would have to reinvent myself to find out what I was all about.

I started this process by blaming myself. When I got involved with the franchise restaurants, the success was so blinding that I was scared of changing anything. I think this is a phenomenon common among business owners.

I was stuck in an ironic rut of success that became a prison in which I was both the prisoner and the warden.

When I saw the brand starting to fail, I blamed myself. I thought I wasn't a good enough operator or that I wasn't pushing myself or my staff hard enough. In retrospect, the high-energy industrial-warehouse feel that worked so well in those first five years had grown stale, and mine weren't the only restaurants to suffer. The brand needed to stay edgy and follow the trends. In my opinion, changing with the times would have meant moving to lighter food, calmer energy and a more wholesome feel. Since the franchise is still in existence today, it's clear that some owners managed to adapt and cater for the next generation of trend-aware customers and that there *were* real solutions.

I was right to blame myself, but I was doing it for the wrong reasons. Blinded by my own arrogance and refusal to fail, I simply couldn't see what was happening. I overstayed my welcome by three years. Had I sold at that point I would have left with really good money and a great history with the brand, but because I was scared stiff of any change, I wasn't able to look at my business objectively.

Ultimately, I was too emotionally involved. The combination of falling into this comfortable rut of success – being afraid of change – and self-blame were dangerous obstacles that I had created for myself.

It isn't unusual to become subjective and emotionally involved in a business. If we don't bring in an objective point of view (for example, a Chief Future Officer) to advise us differently, we are going to carry on doing what we've always done – because it used to work.

The old adage of, 'If it's not broken, don't fix it' does not withstand the test of time. Nothing is unbroken forever – something always eventually breaks or is 'disrupted'.

Why? Because consumer needs and behaviours are constantly changing – and never in human history has the change been as rapid as it is now.

Looking back, I now know that I was not watching the trends and I was not innovating. I hadn't predicted the disruption of our market and I hadn't even reacted to it – except to throw good money after bad. And this determined my downfall. I learnt a lot from that process and the fact that if we don't continuously innovate and watch the trends, we are going to start facing the consequences. Since the days of my *Aghajoon*, things have sped up at such a rate that **we have to be watching new trends on a continuous basis, because there could be a disruptor coming along to knock us off our pedestal at any moment.**

Going through a bankruptcy has taught me so much about what I am doing now: helping businesses to not make the mistakes I made, and to move into the future with purpose and optimism. My methodology and my approach have materialised as consequences of my failure. The crush that I felt after falling from hero to zero was painful and the whole experience forced me to face my emotional self, my personal conflict and my rocky relationship with money.

I became a 'victim' and it took me years to snap out of it; to understand what went wrong and how to build myself up again. I adopted this victim mindset around the age of thirty-two and I stayed there without realising it. I struggled to make money. My internal dialogue was a sad conversation with myself to the tune of: 'Why haven't I made it yet? How come *they've* made it and I haven't? What's wrong with me? What the hell is wrong with the market? Can't they see how amazing I am?'

I was blaming myself, everything and everyone – and I was going nowhere.

Realising this very fact was the start of my transformation. First I had to change my internal voice, then I could focus on a new path to external success

PEEING IN YOUR NAPPY

I use the analogy of 'peeing in your nappy' to describe how self-victimisation becomes familiarity. When you 'pee in your nappy' the first five seconds are amazing: you're nice and warm and you feel relieved – but within a couple of minutes it starts getting cold and it smells and the experience turns horrible.

This is what happens when we start thinking like a victim: the first few seconds are familiar and we feel comfortable in this way of thinking, but soon we find we're heading down a bottomless pit and that we actually hate being there. The initial, perhaps instinctive experience may be rewarding, but you cannot be content with playing a futile blame-game.

Feeling and thinking like a victim are bad habits that we create for ourselves.

Scientists, psychologists and neurologists have extensively researched the intricacies of habits, how they're formed and what sustains or changes them. It's a vast field with far too many studies, findings and theories to mention in detail here, but I will recommend one book: *The Power of Habit: Why we do what we do and how to change* by Charles Duhigg.

Duhigg presents a variety of scenarios that explain the so-called 'habit loop', which is: cue, routine, reward. This loop can be applied to everything, from societies, organisations and sports strategy to consumer habits and addiction.

If a 'victim mindset' is a habit, then there is a cue (or trigger) that ignites victim thought patterns. The habit is the routine that becomes familiar and the reward might be the sense of false security you feel within that victim space.

Our brains like the ease of forming habits and going into auto-pilot; we learn and adapt to respond in a certain way. Regular tasks like driving or washing our hair are habitual and become automated behaviours that, over time, the brain can perform without making an active decision to do so. As a result, our behaviours can become non-intentional acts.

Moreover, habits that are formed unconsciously and without effort often appear to be the most durable.

To change a victim mindset, we would therefore need to create a routine that is enticing enough for us to form a new, meaningful habit.

When the brain is accustomed to thinking in a victim mindset, the process itself becomes a routine that we get trapped into thinking is 'normal' and 'okay'. For me, it was easier to default to a victim mindset because my brain had already habituated this state of mind as my comfort zone.

A personal example: When a friend of mine was chosen to be on the cover of *GQ* magazine, it sent me on an internal tirade of 'Why not me, why him – wtf?!' Instead of being happy for my friend and being inspired by what he had achieved, my reaction was to resent it – and, perversely, my victim mindset took some comfort in this resentment because, *Yes*, I thought, *this is evidence that the world is against me!*

Breaking out of this pattern is as tough as breaking any bad habit and requires continuous work. We have to rewire our brains and keep reminding ourselves to do so, but at times it just feels better to revert back to that familiar place of peeing in your nappy.

I was stuck in a soggy nappy for a long time – until I had an eye-opening experience thanks to a spiritual ritual involving a South American 'teacher plant' known as *ayahuasca*. The plant has been used locally for thousands of years but has only started to gain wider usage around the world as an alternative therapy in the last decade. (It was a profound experience that I highly recommend.) This sojourn into the depths of my mind revealed to me that I had adopted a victim mindset that was overwhelming crucial aspects of my life: money, business and my failing marriage. It was no surprise, then, that I was being defeated in all three. Suddenly, it became clear to me that I was stuck in a bubble of victimhood, and this moment marked the end of a long trek through failure and the beginning of the path that I am on now.

I realised that I had to stop sulking and that all the promising strategies I had built were meaningless without the right mindset. I had been applying all the right methods to my own business, but could not make it work because of my mindset and my emotional approach to money. I started researching, reading books and listening to podcasts to help me figure out what tools I would need in order to change my emotional space.

From the outside, what I had been doing for the previous ten years may have looked great, but that did not determine my reality. While people on the outside were spurring me on and telling me the things I wanted to hear, I was having a different internal dialogue with myself. The external was what everybody could see, but internally I couldn't even see how I was going to make it to the end of the month. It was a familiar dread from my childhood that left me anxious and unable to truly excel.

It took me two years to make sense of and physically get over losing my restaurants, but it took far longer to emotionally recover. When I applied my rational mind, I was able to get back up and give it another try.

Emotionally, however, I was stuck in the victim mindset and I would ultimately spend eight years like this, preventing myself from achieving by keeping my mind in a constrained space.

The minute I steered my emotional space towards success, welcoming money without anxiety and focusing on self-forgiveness and my own self-worth, things took off.

Some time later, in this new phase of my career, I had the best ever financial month since my days as a franchisee. But when the income tapered off the following month, I started having the old conversation with myself: 'I wonder what's going to happen? What if I can't maintain this?' I had to stop myself, set aside the victim mentality, and trust that I was on the right path and that I could keep it up.

Although I would love to travel back in time to tell my twenty-eight-year-old self to: 'Sell now, sell now!' and get out earlier, I would not have built my current businesses without having gone through the perils. Right now, my work is very much based on my *not* getting out early and I am advocating that 'Work is more fun than fun'. People have this idea that fun is about playing a game of bats on the beach or having an ice cream – and those are great activities. But for me, being on stage and talking to a thousand people is just as enjoyable. The idea and concept of fun is not about work; it is about doing something that adds zest to your life, allows you to shine and do what you love – without peeing in your nappy.

THE LONG GAME

All of this allowed me – at the age of forty – to start finding genuine success in my business life (which, of course, involves success in your personal life and is about a lot more than money). I don't claim to offer a magic solution or silver bullet for your problems (I don't believe anyone can), but I do believe that my journey, and the lessons and insights I have learnt along the way, are particularly relevant today. My story exemplifies both the risk of failure and the potential for success in our ever-connected, fast-moving world. If, fifteen years ago, someone had advised me, 'Slow down, look around, start focusing on why you can't love yourself – and follow this advice,' I would have found a short cut around many years of work.

You might be thinking, 'Great! So all I need to do is read this book, apply the tools and then everything will be excellent by tomorrow?' Not so fast. I have some more analogies up my sleeve...

Although I was in an eager rush to get out of my rut, I also had to learn the art of implementing a patient strategy.

The game of cricket has taught me why this works. I am by no means a cricket expert, but I am a keen observer of strategies applied in sports. In top-level cricket there is a one-day game (the One Day International) and a five-day game (Test Cricket).

The one-day game has a limited number of overs, requiring a hard-and-fast approach to achieving the most runs in a single innings. The strategy is generally aggressive, with both teams focusing on the attack. Players are more instinctive and less cautious since time is of the essence.

During the five-day game, team strategies and tactics are prepared much longer (sometimes months) in advance and are applied and adapted with intent throughout the duration of the game. Players must choose wisely when to defend and when to attack with purpose.

In a nutshell, the short game is fast and reckless, while the long game is calculating and strategic.

Importantly, whereas the short game is quickly forgotten, the longer game is considered the truest cricketing format, where the highest form of the sport's success lies.

The point here is not hard to glean: certain things in life need time; the most rewarding form of cricket takes five days; an apple tree needs time to grow; career success is measured over years and decades, not weeks and months.

A plan that plays out over a longer time period requires prudence and patience, and it's where real success lies. When you play the long game to achieve your goals – whether it is in marriage, pursuing an interest or achieving a business plan – you know that success is coming but that it will not be immediate. By adopting a shorter methodology and telling yourself, 'I want it now, it must happen now!', you are trying to force things to happen, and that's where success can turn to failure in the blink of an eye.

Where do these time limits come from? We create them for ourselves with blind impatience. If we can forego the illusion of these time limits and play a long game with a medium- to long-term strategy, we start seeing the bigger picture.

When you try to force a plan to be faster than it is supposed to be, the only thing you're doing is causing stress for yourself and those around you – and compromising your chances of success.

Since discarding my victim mentality and picking myself up, I have become far more accustomed to practising the long game in business (and in my personal life); it is easier, it is calmer, and the decision-making process is not as pressurised. In the past, I would give myself finite deadlines and instantly become tense in any given situation. Even the word 'deadline' creates a gloomy atmosphere as we try to squeeze our energy into getting somewhere as quickly as possible. Watch cricketers play a five-day Test Match: they are calm, they have a strategy on day one, and on day three they have another plan; they know they must be patient and adaptable. In the one-day game they are rushing to get as many runs and wickets as possible and the tension is palpable.

To live life as a one-day player is a fool's game. When I get caught up in the rush of wanting something to happen *now now now*, I actively stop myself and apply the long game. I immediately relax and I no longer feel strangled by deadlines that inhibit my goals.

The biggest challenge that we encounter when attempting to change our mindset is to understand the importance of being aware.

We have to catch ourselves when bad habits take control and blind ambition gets in the way of true achievement.

More importantly, we need replacement tools to negate unconstructive inclinations.

Yogi Bhajan, the spiritual guru who introduced Kundalini yoga, among other things, to the United States, said:

'If you want to learn something, read about it. If you want to understand something, write about it. If you want to master something, teach it.'

Writing this book is my way of mastering the toolsets that I've been using in my talks and workshops – by teaching them.

Yes, I still fall into the traps. I still pee in my nappy from time to time, because it's familiar and comfortable and because it's human nature. It's difficult to overcome those bad habits because they are so ingrained – but it is possible.

Your challenge will be to apply each process and methodology described in this book with the long-game process.

Take your time. Pee in your nappy. Catch yourself and dig your way out. Learn the real meaning of success – then make your success enduring.

CHAPTER TWO

VICTIM?
Understanding the pitfalls of victimhood

Your mindset, habits and internal dialogue can influence your ability to be a successful person – to be a victor. I want to encourage you to truthfully examine the traits that currently define you and think of it as an opportunity to reintroduce yourself – to yourself.

Who are you now and what is holding you back? Who is talking? The victim or the victor?

I believe that everyone has something of a split personality. On one hand, we have a clear image of ourselves: who we are, what our values are and how we present ourselves to the world. On the other hand, we have a voice in our head that is constantly questioning and interrogating our self-image. This voice is at times our best friend, and at times our worst enemy. It has the ability to influence our mindset, and if we don't nurture this friendship and trust the voice, it can shape our mindset into a dark and destructive force.

The yo-yo effect of your inner voice will be hard to ignore in situations where you have to 'put yourself out there'. As a speaker, my inner voice is at its loudest when I am placed on a stage in front of an audience. Either I allow the voice to poke at my self-image and self-esteem and do its best to convince me that the audience is going to find me boring, or I let it tell me that I've got interesting things to say and the crowd is going to enjoy meeting me. The former voice still pops up from time to time to tickle my self-doubt, but that's something I have come to accept and proactively manage.

The best strategy, I have found, is to become aware of which voice is talking to you. Maintain a constant vigilance. The doubting voice might never disappear entirely but it can be soothed, and over time you can transform it into a new voice, as you move from being a victim to being a combination of victim and victor, and eventually to adopting a victor mindset.

Your inner voice influences your self-perception and determines what you project on the outside through, for example, your facial expressions and posture. If you let a self-deprecating voice get the better of you, it can affect the way you show up in the world. When you find yourself sitting on the train or at a conference (or milling about at a drinks party) in a bad mood, complaining to yourself that you can't find a decent job or a new business idea, the frown on your face may be putting off the person next to you, who could well be your new boss or business partner (or friend) – someone you will never connect with because your internal voice is getting the better of you.

In this chapter and the next, I am going to delve into my own interpretations of the different types of victim and victor mindsets, and invite you to listen to the voice inside your head. The point of this chapter is for you to recognise your voice and face its shortfalls. To help you shift your mindset, I will also introduce a practical habit-changing method that can help you guide your inner voice.

The concept of a 'victim and victor' poses a rigid dichotomy: there is a loser and a winner; the weak and the strong. My intention is not to proclaim a deep understanding of the psychology behind personality and behavioural traits that may influence a disposition towards either end of the spectrum, but rather to convey a tangible illustration of the victim and victor characteristics as I have encountered them – in myself and in others. Some of the ideas I present here are not new, but they are a crucial step in the journey towards creating your Moonshot. Think of it like this:

If you don't possess a victor mindset, then how can you even begin to reach your full potential?

MINDSET IS JUST A PATTERN

Before we get into the finer details of the victim and victor traits, we need to answer a question: what is this whole *mindset* thing anyway?

When people ask me how they can change their mindset, I often just say: 'Stop feeling sorry for yourself.' It's not really a fair response, because if it were that simple we'd all just flick a switch in our brains and tune into 'winner mode'. Eckhart Tolle said it more subtly: 'Become the witness to the voice.'

Anyone can change their mindset by being constantly aware of 'the voice' – especially in situations of vulnerability and insecurity. When we become vigilant, we start looking into what this voice is saying, rather than being part of the conversation. At the core of it all, changing your mindset starts with you. Only *you* can reflect on the mindset that you are currently experiencing.

When we wake up in the morning, we essentially have two options. We can either think: 'The day is amazing!' or 'Why do I have to go to work?' I don't believe there is a middle ground because if we don't mind doing something, then we're actually loving it in some way. For me, this needs to be binary. As captains of our own ship, mindset is something that we can commandeer when we make decisions that are not necessarily determined by our character or natural predisposition.

If you are inclined towards being negative (as I was), you will have to work harder and make continuous conscious decisions to think differently. Through your awareness and your own actions, you will be able to detect and prioritise your own mindset, but if you are too lazy to adjust your mindset then you will lose. Long-term success requires constant commitment and dedication to your own cause.

My childhood experience played a major part in shaping my mindset. Raised by a single mother, I didn't have a father figure to pat me on the back, reassure me and 'show me the way'. As a young adult, I started looking for an alpha male father figure, but I never found it. I did, however, end up attracting into my life what I perceived to be male role models, who were emotionally abusive, rather than supportive. My pursuit of acknowledgement was flawed and I had to learn to rid myself of the notion that I needed paternal approval when, in fact, I simply had to approve of myself. Any quest fuelled by desperation or a sense of feeling like a victim is bound to attract abuse or exploitation in one form or another.

In her book, *Mindset: How You Can Fulfil Your Potential,* Dr Carol Dweck writes,

'The view you adopt for yourself profoundly affects the way you lead your life.'

I recommend the book and believe that line pinpoints Dr Dweck's message. Expanding on it, we see that if we believe that our abilities are permanent and cannot be changed, we will perform within the confines of our mindset and the world we have created for ourselves: we will be victims. But if we believe our abilities can change, then opportunities suddenly abound: we will be victors. As victims, we try to prove, but as victors, we try to *im*prove.

This all comes back to the premise that our mindset is a decision. Every time we fail or reach our perceived limits, we can deliberately choose to either retract and remain within our confines, or we can acknowledge the challenge and learn to progress. For long-term success in all walks of life the latter option is essential: we must commit to progress.

First of all, we must become aware of this 'invisible mindset' that we carry with us. Then we must spend the necessary hours, days, weeks and possibly even years focusing on trying to unravel *why* we are, for example, in a victim mindset.

INTERNAL DIALOGUE

If mindset is malleable, we can start to see how it is influenced by our internal dialogue.

Do yourself a favour and take some time to listen to your internal conversations. What tone do you use? Is it a friendly dialogue or are there harsh, self-shaming expletives involved? Ask yourself if you would speak to your best friend the way you speak to yourself.

A key part of realising that I had adopted a victim mindset was the admission to myself that I would never speak to anyone in the tone of my internal dialogue. I realised that I had been verbally abusing myself. When I made a mistake or thought back to something I should have or could have done differently, the tone of my voice was frantic, impatient and unkind.

I chose to become more cautious of the words I used and in doing so it made me more aware of how the voice could affect my behaviour towards others.

I came to realise that when people are nasty to others this is often just a projection of the conversation that is happening inside their heads: it's derogatory and self-abusive.

The discussions we have with ourselves are the most private experiences we can ever have. However, just because our emotions are invisible, we should not be fooled into thinking that they don't matter and that others are oblivious to our thoughts.

What we project on the outside should not define the perception we have of ourselves, because actions are simply not strong enough to disguise what is going on in our heads.

Whatever we do externally – all the brilliance we may lay out for the world to see – cannot overcome low self-esteem and abusive self-talk.

So: we need an emotionally balanced approach in which the outside mirrors the inside.

During my own victim phase, my inner discourse was riddled with anxiety, stress and distrust – but you wouldn't have known it from my outward actions. I was working long hours and operating at capacity, but in my emotional space I wasn't feeling confident. I told myself that I was not achieving and, consequently, my actions and efforts were ultimately fruitless.

In time, I learnt a valuable lesson from a sangoma I consulted. I confided in him about the financial and aspirational problems I was having.

'Oh,' he said, 'it sounds to me as though, in your mind, you believe that hard work is money.'

'That's kind of what we've been taught,' I replied.

Taking my response into account, he then asked me, 'Then why are the guys digging on the side of the road putting in new pipes not the richest people in the world? Surely you can't get harder work than that?'

I knew that he was absolutely right. Hard work doesn't necessarily equal success.

I had tricked myself into thinking that because no-one could hear my internal voice, I could just mask it with effort and eventually success would be mine.

By this stage, I had already figured out I was suffering from self-victimisation, but this insight led me to understand that I had been 'secretly' feeding my victim mindset with the negative drivel that was coming from my internal dialogue.

The problem with trying to be evaluated based on what we project is perfectly described in the saying, 'Don't go broke trying to look rich. Act your wage.' Why do we put on a facade and stretch ourselves thin by buying things to impress the neighbours? Do we really need to buy that expensive pair of jeans (which we don't need) so that other people can think we are wealthy and fabulous? Why are we so bothered about what other people think?

The need for recognition, escapism and personalisation are traits that are common in emerging markets across the world – think of cities like Dubai, Beijing, Kuala Lumpur and Johannesburg. These markets are all underpinned by a mega-trend called 'conspicuous consumption', a term coined by economist and sociologist Thorstein Veblen in the 19th century. It means we spend in order to display economic power, and it leads to buying for the sake of buying. Because emerging markets were all relatively (or disproportionately) poor a generation ago, they are now driven by this trend to 'spend when you can'. (See p134 for more on the emerging awareness market.)

With this in mind, we begin to see that social influences also affect our need to flaunt what we have – to show that we have made it. If I think about it now, buying that video machine as a kid was also motivated by the need to impress others. Yes, I enjoyed watching the videos, but was that *all* I wanted? I think the need to fit in far outweighed the need to be entertained. Even when I didn't have the cashflow to spend frivolously, I tried to maintain an image that supposedly defines wealth.

I have worked hard to remove from my life the desire to buy and show off material things that I don't need. In turn, I've tried to replace it with a desire to be a truer version of myself: somebody who is looking to inspire people and motivate them to also become truer versions of themselves. The image I try to project today is kinder and more 'me' than it ever has been. Not trying to prove anything is the result of working on my internal dialogue. I'm not always able to be humble or to be the quietest person in the room (and for a long time I saw this as a bad thing); I have accepted that I am loud and out there, that I have my own opinions and I'm not shy to share them, unlike many other people.

Self-acceptance starts with acknowledging that you cannot be perfect in everything, but you can be perfect in your own way.

When I was going through my divorce, I felt low and embarrassed about how it affected my image. At the time I confided in a (now late) friend of mine. 'Everyone thinks I'm a dick,' I told him.

He gave me a great piece of advice. 'John, we all are a little bit of a dick and it's okay to own that,' he said.

It was a cathartic statement, and it dawned on me that you can't always be the apple of everyone's eye. You have your good and bad bits, your positives and negatives, and you need to accept and embrace them for what they are to achieve your maximum power.

When I was finally able to project an image that was congruent with my inner dialogue, it was similar to that feeling of emerging from a hot sauna and taking that first gasp of fresh, cool air. That's what it feels like to let go of 'keeping up appearances'.

Moving forward with confidence in yourself means letting go of the small details that obscure your goals, even if it means you won't win the heart of every person you meet along the way.

I recently came across a post on social media that proclaimed, 'Act in a way that if somebody speaks badly of you, the person who is hearing it should say, "That's impossible."' I couldn't agree *less*.

I believe it's far more important to accept that not everybody is going to like you, and that seeking everyone's approval will ultimately hinder your own self-approval. Stop trying to get people to like you and just be who you need to be.

After all, we only need to attract the right people: those who appreciate our mindset, intentions and actions. It's more valuable to belong to a 'tribe' that understands you than to try to fit into a universal persona that pleases everyone's ideals.

The point is: mindset can't be ignored. Before you start any important actions, you need to run a self-check to assess your own attitude towards yourself. If you already possess an inkling of the right (victor) mindset, you'll need to use fewer tools as you move forward, but focusing on your mindset will always get you into a space that allows you to flourish. When your attitude is right, you approach things from the stance of, 'Wow, there are opportunities everywhere,' rather than, 'Why haven't I made it yet? I wish I had been raised differently. Why didn't I study harder at university?'

When you get your own mindset right, you start seeing the opportunities more clearly, and the means to achieve soon follow.

FACING YOUR OWN VICTIM

It is possible, as my experiences attest, to be a victor who was once a victim. The reverse is also true, and for those like me who have taken the journey from victim to victor the danger of slipping back into old habits is real. For me, being able to recognise the process as it's happening has been integral to staying on the victor track.

In order to reap the benefits of harnessing a victor mindset, we need to actively shape our way of thinking. If we can pinpoint what it's like to be a victim, then we can identify that feeling as it arises and take steps to carve our way out of that mindset – even if it has to be an ongoing exercise.

We need to challenge ourselves by taking a long hard look at the typical victim traps and honestly recognising whether or not we have succumbed to them in the past.

In many ways, our mindset is informed by behaviour and habits that are shaped and acquired throughout life.

We learn by doing things over and over again – and if habits are formed by learning, this suggests we can also unlearn our victim mindset.

When you find yourself in victim mode, it's up to you to press pause and analyse the specifics of the situation. You'll often find you're seeking the approval of others or blaming others rather than accepting yourself as is.

Let's take a closer look at the victim personas to look out for. Your task will be to see if you can identify with any – or all – of the characteristics described.

In my experience, there are three types of victims: the Martyr Victim, the Arrogant Superior Victim and the Arrogant Inferior Victim. I have come across each type in myself or in others and flagged the accompanying traits as 'victim traps'. If you can relate to any of these, you will have made the first step towards setting up your internal alert system.

The Martyr Victim

Martyr Victims possess the following key traits. They –

1. sacrifice personal ambitions in the perceived belief that others are benefiting as a result;
2. resent the sacrifices they have made in servitude of others;
3. find solace in playing a role they believe is akin to martyrdom;
4. publicly proclaim/advertise their own sacrifices;
5. are easily dominated or bullied into thinking they are inferior;
6. feel painfully sorry for themselves and blame themselves or others;
7. make their apparent beneficiaries aware of the sacrifices they have made;
8. can be passive aggressive and easily 'disgusted' by people or situations.

When we fall into a role that we unwillingly accept as our destiny, we are acting as Martyr Victims.

An obvious example of this type is the traditionally minded housewife who plays a predetermined role within her culture and 'sacrifices' her own ambitions as a result. She may accept that this is where she belongs, but as resentment creeps in she tries to justify it with the idea that she is being a martyr for the benefit of others.

Being a walkover and fitting into a mould can turn even those with the best intentions into a Martyr Victim. This is not to say that a working mother who gives up a dream job as a travelling journalist and takes on a 9-to-5 office job instead is a Martyr Victim.

We all make small sacrifices in life to accommodate and offer a compromise for the needs of others, but there must be a clear understanding of why we are giving something up, and whether or not doing so makes us happy.

Thinking that it will please others is not good enough if we can't live without regretting the forfeitures or if the recipients and beneficiaries of our 'sacrifices' are acutely aware of and affected by our resentment. Resentment can show up in the form of passive aggressive behaviour and eventually as feelings of anger and disgust.

A victim and a martyr are opposite sides of the same coin. What do we think of when we hear the word 'martyr'? A saint or heroic figure? Someone who has made a great, benevolent and selfless sacrifice for the benefit of others? It's easy to idolise martyrs when we compare them to our own human flaws, but real martyrdom is a rare occurrence. As a true martyr, there is no need for reward or recognition. The greatest kind of philanthropist and altruist, for instance, does not give publicly. On the opposite end, an egoist will do good in an attempt to gain public recognition and approval – a personal and selfish sense of achievement. The point is that we can't justify victimhood by trying to be a martyr.

I grew up in an environment in which making an abundance of money came with a certain sense of guilt; I felt like I could not enjoy success *and* a sense of integrity at the same time. As I explored this inner conflict, I realised that even if I tried to be more like a magnanimous martyr, I would not necessarily be immune to certain victim traits. Self-sacrifices that are of no benefit to us or to those around us can potentially spawn a victim mindset.

The Arrogant Superior Victim

Arrogant Superior Victims possess the following key traits. They –

1. shamelessly bully, control and berate others;
2. are angry about factors that apparently prevent their own greatness;

3 passively deal with issues;

4 prefer conflict over diplomacy;

5 use blame as a tool to justify and mask feelings of inferiority;

6 find solace in blaming extraneous factors for their misfortune;

7 are constantly on the defensive and mask this behaviour as a form of attack.

When it comes to Arrogant Superior Victims, small actions can speak volumes. Their behaviour is so far removed from a victor's actions and nature that they are pretty easy to spot.

This type of victim is trying to (or pretending) to be a victor.

Personal examples

I used to work with a client who ran a business valued at over a billion rand. One day I was waiting in the boardroom to start a session with him and his team. He arrived early and walked straight past the head of the table and sat next to me in the middle of the table. I asked why he wasn't sitting at the head of the table, to which he responded, 'I avoid the head of the table at all costs.' To me, this was indicative of him being a victor in his mindset and not needing to prove his authority.

Another previous client of mine – who ran a R100-million business – displayed the complete opposite approach: he would always sit at the head of the table with his arms behind his head, leaning back in his chair and allowing everybody in the boardroom to talk before he did. This was his way of applying some of the supposed rules of leadership, but once everyone had been heard, he inevitably berated and called out his staff, mentioning how inferior their ideas were and then presenting his own opinions as the unquestionable solution. When things didn't go according to (his) plan, he would get angry about it. Through his anger, those around him lost their ability to be creative. He was being an Arrogant Superior Victim in his approach, disguising insecurity by sitting at the head of the table, arms over his head and exuding arrogant superiority.

A good example of an Arrogant Superior Victim is someone who tends to be a bully. Dominating and berating others is their feeble attempt at being a victor. A real victor does not need to bully.

It's a fake victory. Their internal voice is that of a victim and putting somebody else down is their way of feeling superior.

What's happening here? Emotionally, the Arrogant Superior Victim is staying poor by trying to get rich. In this mindset, the victim might be inclined to thinking: 'Everybody is an idiot.'

He is angry about what's going on and doesn't even question the reasons behind his own anger, because it gives him the distorted sense of security that comes with peeing in his nappy. Outcries might include, 'The bloody government is hopeless!' and 'I can't travel abroad because the exchange rate is so bad!' For him, the grass is always greener on the other side.

Regular anger and a sense of empowerment from looking down on everyone and everything that doesn't meet your standards and satisfaction may not seem obvious indicators of victimhood – and yet they are. The mask the Arrogant Superior Victim wears allows him to access an interior language that only consists of superior blame and feelings of resentment, antagonism, hate and discrimination.

Arrogant Inferior Victim

Arrogant Inferior Victims possess the following key traits. They –

1. are easily threatened by those who are perceived as superior in comparison to themselves;

2 defend their own position and inferiority in order to feel secure;

3 are quick to deem opinions of others as 'nonsense' when they don't fit into their own opinions;

4 find comfort in the apparent faults of others;

5 often give up before they have even started;

6 are unlikely to ever read a book like this or take in any new and fresh perspectives.

The most dangerous mindset that I have come across (and suffered from) is that of the Arrogant Inferior Victim. This type of victim arrogantly presumes that anyone who is doing better than them is in fact a crook, wrong and/or stupid. This mindset justifies the inferiority that is felt when we compare ourselves to others who are (perceived to be) more fortunate, more attractive or more successful.

A personal example: A former colleague of mine unintentionally introduced me to the concept of an Arrogant Inferior Victim and made me realise that I too had been harbouring this type of victim in my secret headspace. Like many stories, this one begins with love. My colleague fell in love with a wonderful woman who happened to be particularly wealthy. He hadn't ever been very financially successful himself, but love prevailed. Soon enough they were married. When they moved to a beautiful upmarket coastal suburb, he slipped into a luxurious lifestyle that he had never really experienced before. Most of us would say he was a pretty lucky guy: he got the woman he loved and she was able to afford them financial security and a dream house.

A few months after their wedding I called him up to see how he was doing. He spent the duration of our conversation expressing how irritated he was by the well-heeled people in his new neighbourhood. Not once did he pause to acknowledge the benefits that his new environment undoubtedly afforded him. Instead, he lambasted the 'rich mommies in their SUVs' and complained endlessly about how terrible it all was. I almost felt sorry for him, until it dawned on me that he was playing the victim.

This characterises a victim in the worst situation. He's not just a victim who feels sorry for himself; he is arrogantly justifying why everyone around him is pathetic and how he deserves better. How can he ever be prosperous if he is stuck in a 'poor me' mindset? For someone like him, being a victim is already bad enough on its own, but the arrogance and state of inferiority confounding this demolish him because he justifies staying in his victim state. He feels vindicated and warrants his bad attitude by proclaiming that 'all rich people are idiots' and he doesn't even want to be there – which is like being victim version 2.0.

Just because someone may think he is superior that doesn't mean he's winning. It's actually a terrible place to be, because he (thinks he) is surrounded by fools.

When you hear someone say, 'Everybody is an idiot', the truth is that not everyone is an idiot; that's just the way he is perceiving the world to be. The Arrogant Inferior Victim's language consists of blame and his mindset displays a total lack of power and inferiority: he feels lost, hopeless, defeated and unenthusiastic.

If we are *blaming* anybody and everybody for what's happening in our lives, then we are in one of the victim modes, really. It is as simple as that.

'Why haven't I made it yet?' Blaming.

'Why am I not being recognised for my efforts?' Blaming.

'Why is the economy so bad?' Blaming.

'Why is the government not doing more?' Blaming.

It's time to stop playing that broken record.

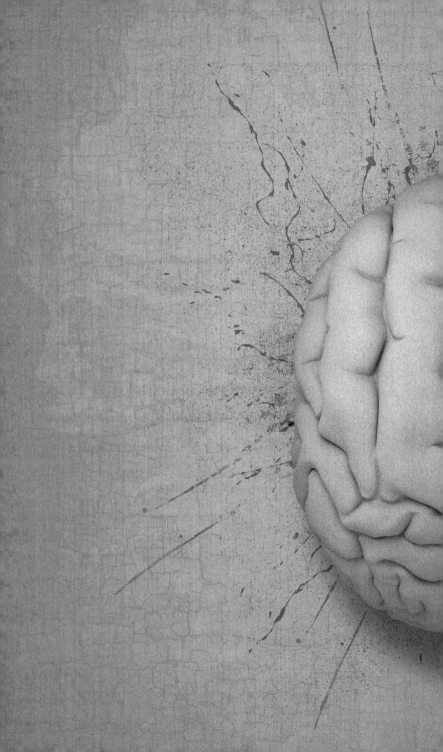

CHAPTER THREE

VICTOR!
Forging a winning mindset

Three simple words: *Just Do It*. There's a reason why the Nike slogan epitomises the brand's image of success, achievement and victory. They encourage you to stop overthinking, stop hesitating and just go for it – go for the win. After the previous chapter, these victor qualities should come as a breath of fresh air.

A victor is someone who **doesn't take things personally.**

For me, that's one of the strongest traits of the victor mindset. The world is *not* out to get you, so don't let a setback get you down. When we are victors we see opportunity everywhere, and if we hear a knock on the door we're not afraid to answer it. If it doesn't work out, that's okay, because there is another door just around the corner. But note: there's a difference between listening to the knock on the door and getting up and going to answer it.

A victim will conjure up the effort to predetermine that they are going to be turned down. That way, when they are in fact turned down, they can say, 'I told you so.' The victor, on the other hand, will say, 'No problem. Next?' It's such a simple example of the choice we have. Someone else's opinion of us – or being turned down – doesn't matter when we are just moving from opportunity to opportunity.

In his analysis of what makes new habits more steadfast, Pulitzer Prize-winning author Charles Duhigg makes mention of how belief (in a group, community, religion or purpose) is a powerful factor that can help retain a new or replaced habit. If we consider that changing from a victim to a victor mindset means adopting new habits to support our outlook, then belief – not entitlement – is a central component to maintaining victor traits.

A friend of mine once told me that we have an epidemic of entitled people in the world. It was the first time I had ever encountered this idea, and as I listened to him it dawned on me that I myself felt entitled. I had this idea that things should just automatically work.

That subtle 'entitlement-expectation' freezes us and renders us inept, because we are expecting and waiting for some kind of amazing privilege to reveal itself 'any moment now...' It's an Arrogant Superior Victim trait that causes us to sit around and wait for our dues to arrive. But that's not how reality works.

If you have a dream, it must be backed up by a victor mindset and an active search for opportunities to achieve that dream.

If you think, 'Well, I've put my dream out into the universe so why hasn't it happened yet?', you will wait to fulfil your dream until the cows come home – if they ever do – because even cows don't like victims.

A personal example: I'll use my friend Mark to illustrate the difference between entitlement and belief. I call Mark the 'King of Audaciousness' because, to my knowledge, he doesn't have a single strain of DNA in his body that makes him feel bad or rejected.

The tale starts with him as a little kid: eight years old and chubby as a cherub. Mark developed a crush on the prettiest girl in class so, being the King of Audaciousness, he boldly approached her for her hand in courtship. To which she replied: 'No, you're fat.'

The automatic reaction of almost anyone who hears this story is pity for the poor little child who poured his heart out and was turned down on such superficial grounds. Not Mark. From his perspective, for the first time in his life, he realised that 'fat equals undesirable'.

Mark didn't get upset. Instead, he chose to start losing weight. Incredibly, he dropped from 80kg to a far healthier 50kg that very year, and he later thanked his offender for pointing out his problem. As the King of Audaciousness, being a victor just comes naturally to him; he appears to have been 'designed' that way.

Mark is an extreme example and most of us won't enjoy that natural predisposition. If the pretty girl had told the eight-year-old me that I was fat, I would have felt rejection, become depressed and eaten *more* doughnuts – in fact, I think I would still do that...

> **The lesson here is that the belief of being a victor is greater than the feeling of being entitled to victory.**

If we're not born with it, we have to train ourselves to believe that we can be victors. So when we are being told we are inadequate, how do we deal with it? If we are dealing with it by thinking, 'I am entitled to be however I want to be without criticism!' we are being victims. If we are victors who are comfortable with being overweight, then comments about our physique are like water off a duck's back. However, if we see room for improvement, we go ahead and make some changes, because we *believe* that we can. We believe that we are – or can be – the best version of ourselves.

If we believe in ourselves and our abilities, then we don't have (or need) a sense of entitlement. We never ask, 'Why is this not happening?' We find opportunities and ask, 'What's next?'

VICTOR TRAITS

The first step to a victor mindset is to realise that you are in victim mode.

When presented with this notion, arrogant and entitled victims might think, 'No, that's not me. I'm a victor. I know better already.' They are suffering and will never find a solution because they are too afraid to face themselves.

Victors possess the following key traits. They –

1. see and find opportunities everywhere;
2. don't rely on their outside projection to the world (or image) to secure their worth;
3. focus on success, not failure;
4. move through the world with irreverence and a sense of humanity;
5. see everyone as equals.

There are three ways in which we can look at the world: being judged, judging or seeing everyone in the world as an equal. I have looked at the world in all three of these ways and, admittedly, I sometimes still lean towards the first two – we are all human, after all (which is why conscious effort is so important for personal growth).

To understand the core of a victor, we can compare it to the three victim types: the Martyr Victim and Arrogant Inferior Victim think they are always being judged, while the Arrogant Superior Victim looks at the world through superior eyes, judging and looking down on others. When we judge or feel judged, we automatically limit our opportunity to learn from others.

By contrast, the victor reserves judgement in favour of seeing others as equals in order to access unlimited opportunities and potential in everyone and everything.

'Some animals are more equal than others,' said George Orwell in *Animal Farm*. He was making a valid point about the nature of the world, and I think the hardest part of buying into the victor mindset is the idea of seeing everyone as an equal. If you are in a leadership position, or you are a business owner, you tend to command a certain amount of power. This power is not something that makes you perceivably 'equal' to others. For example, you may be regarded as superior when you earn a bigger salary than your employees, making them 'less equal' by default.

But if you can grant yourself the ability to see everyone you interact with as your equal, you open up endless possibilities that are not blocked by preconceived opinions; you don't discriminate against anyone who is above or below you and you look at everyone as having an equal amount of potential.

If you want to be a victor and achieve your Moonshot, your personal goal should be to **learn how you can approach life with a sense of 'interiority'.**

INTERIORITY AND EQUANIMITY

Interiority *noun*: the quality of looking inward; the ability to look at everyone as an equal, rather than from a point of superiority or inferiority – *important for inner character and reflection*

Equanimity *noun*: mental composure, particularly the retention of power and poise when faced with adversity – *important for holding an objective outlook and controlling the influences of the external world*

As we have seen, our internal dialogue can produce a cacophony of thoughts that cloud our ability to figure out what we should be tuning into or focusing on. A wonderful way to direct our internal voice so that it's coming from the right place is to look at the world with *interiority*. Unlike superiority and inferiority, this is not about comparing ourselves with others; it's about finding contentment from within. We should avoid considering other people as good or bad because that means we are judging ourselves as either being good or bad in return. When we spend time judging others – or ourselves – we end up dispersing our energy and power. When nobody around us is good or bad and we withhold judgement of others, we gain true power – and empowerment.

Interiority allows us to bring our whole, full power into a space where everybody is equal and everybody offers an opportunity.

We all know someone who is 'larger than life'. Someone simply incredible and capable of achieving anything. The reason these people seem larger than life is because they approach the world with interiority. They don't waste energy by judging, looking down on and blaming others, or looking up and thinking they aren't good enough. Interiority says: 'We are all here together – let's have a party and actually do this.'

Is it impossible to stop judging others? We can be inclined to judge based on what society, our family and our beliefs have told us. If our environment has influenced our patterns of thinking, we have to fracture the way we have been programmed by shifting our internal language and inner dialogue. Just because our perceptions have been shaped to be how they are at this point in our lives, that doesn't mean we mustn't or are unable to shift the pattern. *How* we think is a belief system in itself – and we can believe whatever we choose to believe.

A personal example: I used to have a friend whose family was devoutly religious and went by the premise that religion and money don't mix, especially 'easy money'. I remember his grandmother saying to me, 'People of our faith never win the lottery because that is not God's way. You must work hard for your money.'

With respect to his grandmother and her religion – and the merits of playing the lottery aside – this particular outlook is not a winning mindset because it justifies the self-sacrifice of victimhood and it judges people who choose not to live as martyrs. Moreover, it makes it exceptionally difficult to balance your faith and ambitions in life because a person who truly followed this line of thinking would inevitably compromise any ambition to succeed in the long run. As victors, we can be humble and still remain true to our faith or beliefs.

A victor with interiority adopts a language that consists of phrases like, 'Wow, there are so many opportunities out there!' and 'What more can I learn right now to improve myself?' and 'What can I *do*?'

A real victor will always think, 'How can I make this work?'

The ability to accept challenges with grace is a virtue that can be defined as *equanimity*. Yes, it's quite a mouthful. Metaphorically speaking, it means that our emotional state should be like water: going with the flow and trusting the flow so much that we are level-headed about whatever is coming towards us. Equanimity means that we can find calm and stability under strained circumstances. It allows us to always ask ourselves, 'Am I being objective about what I believe should or shouldn't happen?' There is no point in falling prey to our circumstances. There is no value in hanging our heads and weeping at lost prospects when we could be looking for other fish to fry.

We are tested to practise equanimity and acceptance every day when we are exposed to melodrama and information that does not serve a real purpose, often through mainstream media. CNN – 'Crisis News Network' – and other running news channels love to feed our victim mindsets. And, of course, so much of social media abounds in self-involved victimhood. The more bullshit we open our ears and eyes to, the more we think it's okay to be like that. I strongly recommend to anyone reading this to upgrade yourself by avoiding mainstream news and unnecessary online interactions; as an alternative, try listening to podcasts by thought leaders who can enrich your lives and get you out of your nappies.

Drama can be addictive because our 'fight or flight' response kicks in and makes us keep up our guard.

We get used to feeling the rush we get from hearing about others' dilemmas and trying to keep up with what everyone is talking about. Some people appear to thrive on drama or stress and adopt a mentality along the lines of: 'If you're not stressing or working hard then you are not winning or making money.' If you can find an environment or lifestyle in which you can prioritise your emotions over everything else, you will realise that you can be happy and productive without spinning on a hamster wheel until you run out of energy.

By filtering out complaints and the urge to judge, we are best able to find a space where we can alter the ingrained patterns that subtly govern our mindset. We can recruit interiority and equanimity to help us steer our internal dialogue and think like a victor.

The Victor Toolset

Things to remember if you want to be a victor:

1. Follow your highest excitement.
2. Show up with maximum enthusiasm.
3. Know what sort of outcome you want.
4. Let go of the exact picture of how it needs to turn out, and trust the process.
5. Catch yourself when you complain.
6. Catch yourself when the voice in your head starts talking 'superior' or 'inferior' nonsense.

THE ART OF IRREVERENCE

Irreverence *noun*: lack of respect for people or situations that are usually taken seriously; positive trait when used to bypass negative opinions and thoughts – *the ultimate superpower when used positively*

To clarify the dynamics of the victim and victor types, it's important to also consider the concept of irreverence, which is formally defined as 'a lack of respect for people or things that are generally taken seriously'. When applied selectively, it can be a compelling trait.

As an example, when everyone is ranting about obnoxious politicians, you might choose an irreverent approach towards this increasingly frequent topic of (heated and often boring) conversation. Yes, the politics themselves may be important, but the conversations – or, more likely, the shouting matches – about them generally are not; people have just convinced themselves to *think* they are.

Irreverence allows you to laugh off the question, tell a joke, change the topic, talk about something that's genuinely interesting. Irreverence can therefore also indicate that we don't buy into social constructs that become obstacles in our pursuit of victor habituation. This may smell an awful lot like arrogance, but there is a difference between being *irreverent and warm* (confident), and *irreverent and cold* (arrogant).

Arrogant irreverence makes us single-minded and focused on our own success, regardless of what we do and how we do it. In fact, it doesn't even allow us to treat ourselves that well, because it makes us cold towards ourselves too. We happily squeeze everything out of other people who can contribute to our own gain and we maximise our own profit. We go in for the short kill and tend to be manipulative. I was coldly irreverent when I was financially successful and running my restaurants: I didn't care what anybody thought; I was blissfully irreverent and successful – but I was *arrogant*.

If, however, we can maintain confident, warm irreverence, it offers an all-encompassing and collaborative energy. We don't buy into all the superfluous rubbish that goes on around us, and when people start complaining and putting problems on a pedestal we prefer to subtly change the subject.

After my bankruptcy I stopped being (arrogantly) irreverent and became the very opposite: a people-pleaser. In this Inferior Victim mindset, I neglected my own priorities while wanting to make everyone around me happy. I was custard. I couldn't achieve anything genuinely positive or get my own way when I really needed to. The idea that I had to please others all of the time was a killer.

Trying to please everybody is like running on a treadmill that keeps getting faster and faster until you fall off.

In my mind, I was trying to be like Gandhi. I wanted to be the kinder, better person – which certainly has its benefits – but eventually I fell off that treadmill and hit reality. The minute I snapped into a victor mindset again, the power of irreverence returned. I started thinking, 'If you don't like it, that's your baby.' With irreverence on my side, I *can* be kind, but I won't *always* be kind; I *can* be friendly, but I won't *always* be friendly – and that's okay. No more custard.

(It was only later that I learnt more about Gandhi: that he was not entirely flawless and that he knew how to bring his positive aspects to the fore to achieve his goals. Gandhi believed in passive resistance but he was no-one's victim.)

Incorporating warm irreverence into my life was a critical step in embracing the victor mindset.

The practice of warm irreverence can be a superpower because it helps us to focus on solutions without incorporating futile discussions into our daily thinking.

It is a characteristic of the long-term approach because it allows us to laugh off fleeting unimportant concerns. As a victor, we don't care what everybody else thinks and it becomes a natural inclination to stop focusing on the details that don't add any real value to our lives.

Warm irreverence, which is synonymous with 'charisma', is also a wonderful way to move people. *The Charisma Myth* by Olivia Fox Cabane argues that charisma is, in fact, a behavioural technique that can be learnt by anyone.

Charisma consists of three characteristics: presence, power and warmth.

Being *present* is perhaps the most obvious element: a charismatic person is someone who genuinely engages with other people. And it seems straightforward enough, in theory, as it essentially boils down to not thinking about something else when we are interacting with others. Yet it's easy to let our minds drift to a story we want to tell – often about ourselves – or the response we want to give, with the result that we stop really listening. Being present, and thus having presence, is a commitment to giving someone else the stage.

Of course, to be charismatic we need to be able to take the stage when it's our time, and showing *power* is a similarly important piece of the pie. Someone who has presence but no power simply becomes a walkover. We need to engage with conviction; if we yield too easily and let people have their way, we will act against our will and resent giving in just to please others. Charisma is irresistible when we know what we want and have a tender way of getting it.

We can practise irreverence with the two elements of presence and power alone, but it's the all-important *warmth* that elevates irreverence to genuine charisma, and in so doing avoids the pitfall of arrogance. Warmth confers sincerity and approachability; it shows that we care about what someone else has to say without passing judgement.

Today, I happily think of myself as a confident, irreverent victor (most of the time) and I often remind myself that true confidence comes across in a warm manner when we act with integrity. It's a place where we would rather empower others than look down on them.

The art of irreverence lies in not being distracted by the clutter of outside perceptions, but being selective about what really matters, and giving yourself the freedom and confidence to be a victor.

STEERING YOUR INTERNAL DIALOGUE TO CHANGE YOUR MINDSET

Once you've taken those important first steps of identifying your personal victim or victor traits – and taken on board the ideas of interiority, equanimity and the art of irreverence – you can start committing to the process of ingraining new thought patterns into your daily life. The intention is to change your mindset to one that prioritises your happiness and maintain a long-term perspective: to become a victor.

For example, if a client cancels a meeting five minutes before you are due to meet, you have a quick decision to make: you can be the victim of the situation and blame the client for being so inconsiderate, or you can respect the client's circumstances and see the situation as an opportunity to go for a walk or take a break and clear your head. It's often as easy as that.

Of course, you don't want to be a walkover, and you can in time express your dissatisfaction (in a kind way), but the priorities when encountered with this type – and almost any type – of situation are: *How do I remain happy? How do I channel equanimity?*

Happiness is a broad emotion generally associated with specific emotions and actions. By identifying the emotions and actions that generate our personal happiness, as well as the corollary emotions and actions that generate our unhappiness, we can start working out a practical plan to prioritise our happiness. The key is to focus on the habits that lead to these emotions and actions because habits are generally unthinking, triggered by cues that we are not necessarily aware of. We tend to learn habits unconsciously, and over time they become routine; routine then guides our actions and emotions, and ultimately our general state of happiness.

The point is: habits don't worry about our feelings in the moment, but they affect them in the long run. So we need to actively change our habits to change our mindset and our long-term happiness.

This process in itself becomes a positive habit that removes us from the state of being a victim and connects us with our emotions, intentions, goals and desires.

If we dabble with some of these tactics and they don't meaningfully affect us, we have to conclude that the victim mode is still governing our thoughts; that we are being ruled by emotions that we cannot control. We need to change our internal dialogue – that process we think nobody can see but which we in fact project to the world – so that we can self-correct towards being a better version of ourselves. Once we reach the tipping point, we don't need to look back.

To make this process less conceptual and more practical, I would like to introduce a tool that anybody can apply by returning to the work of Charles Duhigg, which offers a feasible framework to shifting and reshaping habits. Since there is no guaranteed formula for changing habits, *we* need to bring the main ingredients to the party: effort, experimentation and endurance.

I have used an interpretation of Duhigg's model, as presented by behavioural psychology specialist James Clear, to define a three-step process that is relevant in the context of changing the mindset from one that is steered by victim patterns to one that is governed by victor patterns. Clear calls this framework 'The 3 Rs of habit change', but I prefer to add 'mindset' to the name to emphasise the active mental aspect of what we're doing.

THE 3 Rs OF CHANGING MINDSET HABITS

The 3 Rs are: Reminder, Routine, Reward. Let's look at them in more detail before implementing action plans to bring them into our lives. (Note that the starting point for action is, in fact, the final R – Reward.)

1 Reminder

The reminder is the start of the change: it is the out-of-the-ordinary alert telling you to enforce a new habit (which becomes a routine).

The fabled 'golden rule of habit change', which has been proven to work in countless studies, explains that 'you can't extinguish a bad habit, you can only change it'. So before you can shape a new habit you need to pinpoint the current reminder – or cue – that's setting off your existing habit loop. What's triggering your routines and making you pee in your nappy?

This isn't meant to be an aggressive process. When the cue arrives, you need to establish how you feel about it. How can you become more aware of the cue that triggers your routine, so that you can act on it?

Perhaps your cue for bad eating habits and resulting bad health and exercise routines is feeling hungry. So what do you do? Without really thinking about it, you walk to the fridge to get something to eat. When you have made a decision to prioritise weight loss and getting fit, you need a reminder to tell you 'Don't forget!' every time the cue comes knocking. This can be a note on the fridge that says CARROTS TASTE LIKE CHOCOLATE! or a daily reminder, such as a 5am alarm, telling you to get up and go to gym (and think about your eating choices). The minute this reminder comes up, it should act as a trigger to change your mindset.

A personal example: Every (working) day, the first thing I look at in the morning is the calendar pop-up that is programmed to appear on my phone at a certain time. I put myself into the emotional state that those reminders represent for my routines that will arise during the course of the day. Every time I see them, I am able to move forward after I have been reminded (again) about what I want to prioritise.

I also write messages to myself on the mirrors at home as hints that keep triggering the thoughts that I want to adopt. These are my cues to start the day with the right mindset.

ACTION: Work out what your cues are and what reminders you can implement for those that you want to change.

2 Routine

Now that the reminder has alerted you to the impending habit/routine, it's time to change the routine.

Start by identifying up to five bad habits that you want to change and then define your routine and the ritual that will allow you to implement new good habits to replace them on a daily, weekly or monthly basis.

You can set your reminders in whatever way you want, but it's crucial that you have a clear plan for your new routine; when the reminder comes, you need to know what you're going to do and exactly how you're going to achieve it. The reminder to wake up at 5am might lead to the routine of getting to the gym at 6am because your personal trainer is waiting there for you.

Creating routines is probably the biggest challenge to changing habits since they have to be viable alternatives to the existing routines that are keeping you in the victim trap. You've worked out the cues and set your reminders – but it's easy to ignore a reminder or to start overlooking it if the new routine doesn't satisfy you.

You may also start resenting the reminder because it becomes an admonition of what you have *not* achieved. That's when you must apply the long game.

When we rush things, we put pressure on ourselves to meet unrealistic targets, and we end up scolding ourselves when we don't achieve our goals. We need to talk to ourselves as friends. Rather say, 'You know, that's so funny. A part of me still falls into victim mode' than, 'Damn it, I'm in victim mode again! What's wrong with me?' The latter is the short-term approach, whereas the long game allows us to calmly recognise when we have missed the mark, and just keep going.

The most important thing about managing your internal voice is maintaining self-respect.

We may think that we have to punish ourselves in order to improve, but we don't. That's when we never improve. We have to be pulled towards where we want to be; an unkind internal voice only drives us away.

When we hate something we reject it, and when we love something we are drawn to it.

A personal example: At one stage I would look at myself in the mirror and think, 'Wow, I'm fat. I shouldn't have eaten that chocolate cake last night – that whole chocolate cake!' To change my internal conversations like this, I had to consciously allow myself to modify my thinking patterns and I created complimentary behavioural changes, such as exercising every morning. I was able to get into the routine of saying, 'I love you, my body. I want you to be amazing.' It took me a while to be able to commit to this feeling – and not eating chocolate every day helped too – but by habitualising this self-respect, I was able to influence a 'normal' response to certain aspects of myself.

ACTION: Swap your existing negative routines for new positive routines with realistic goals.

3 Reward

Well done. You've worked out your cues and set your reminders, and you've started new routines that are delivering results. Now: reward yourself!

As soon as you accomplish one of your goals, you need to pat yourself on the back and feel good about it. Victims believe that self-reward is a bad idea, but victors know that anyone deserves reward for success, including themselves. The very act of successfully changing a negative routine is worthy of a reward.

If you are making the effort to train at 6am, five days a week, your short-term reward may be a delicious smoothie after each workout. Your long-term reward may be that you can confidently step out in a swimsuit on the beach in summer – do it!

Note, however, that the sense of reward may be misleading and/or short-term, and that bad habit loops often conclude with these false rewards. For example, checking your phone every time it pings may give you a sense of satisfaction ('reward'), which has created the habit loop – but it's generally a bad habit worth breaking.

Identifying the reward that satisfies your bad habits is just as important as identifying the cue that triggered it. Similarly, **your new habits must have clear reminders and clear rewards.**

The key here is to maintain your success even when the outlook is not at its best. Enter the concept of 'victory conditions'. I've borrowed this term from the world of gaming. It describes the conditions that must be met in order to win a game; in other words, victory conditions determine how we win the game. There is usually more than one victory condition that we need to fulfil before we can win. The same applies to rewarding ourselves, because we need to set victory conditions for every success – no matter how big or small – to keep us motivated throughout our pursuit of the end-goal.

Hiking up the mountain or walking on the beach with your dog at 3pm on a weekday may be a victory condition for you to be enjoying your work (it is for me). Sourcing and eating the best food you can find may be a victory condition for you being happy with your health and body. Travelling to a dream destination – victorious for almost anyone. Victory conditions are there so you can avoid forever chasing your own tail.

The rewards need to be something that you allow yourself to do, and whether that's a daily gesture or a massive bonus you give yourself is up to you. The objective will always remain the same: to do something for yourself in exchange for the self-investment you have made. It's a win-win, really.

A crucial point to note now is that **you need to map out your victory conditions before you start setting your reminders** and forming new routines so that, when you do make progress, you can celebrate your accomplishments. And you certainly need to celebrate those accomplishments, because if you don't then you won't really be achieving anything.

ACTION: Ask yourself: 'What are my victory conditions and when do I know I am being victorious?' Outline practical rewards that you can give yourself at every stage of every routine that you are seeking to change that will lead you to your victory conditions.

CONNECTING THE DOTS

The questions you should be asking yourself as we head towards the end of the chapter are:

1 Am I inferior, superior or interior?
2 Am I a victim or a victor?
3 Am I feeling entitled or do I believe in my own worth?
4 Am I going to create?

Every day, our inner dialogue may go through various phases of superiority and inferiority, but only by truthfully monitoring our internal language will we be able to improve. By working out what our victim and victor traits are, we can ascertain what needs to be done to overcome the former and enhance the latter.

It's hard work to become aware of our inner dialogue, but it's harder work when we're on the hamster wheel and we're not going anywhere.

It might initially require a lot of effort to think differently, but the point is we need to *become aware* and then figure out what our options are.

Changing mindset habits is not necessarily a peaceful process, and it's even more stressful if we are at odds within ourselves and defending ourselves against outside judgement. Protecting old habits could make us resort to anger as a defence mechanism. It's like being the kid who didn't get sweets and throws a tantrum: it's habitual; it's peeing in your nappy. And it doesn't help in that moment or in the long run. That kid grows up but the behaviours can remain; if he doesn't get his way he hides in a sulk bubble.

To rid ourselves of blame, we need to 'grow up'. If we don't, the people close to us, whether colleagues or family, business or life partners, are often the people we act out towards when we don't get our sweets.

But we don't grow up by trying to predict the future; we grow up by reviewing the past and accepting the present. If we try to figure everything out in advance, we will find ourselves stuck trying to make everything fit and be perfect. In reality, we may only realise why things happened the way they did with the hindsight of time. Steve Jobs said it perfectly: 'We can't connect the dots looking forward; we can only connect them looking backwards. So we have to trust that the dots will somehow connect in our future.'

This means we should be looking at the dots behind us to understand how they end up connecting, and worry less about making all the 'right' decisions now that may get us stuck trying to piece together a puzzle that doesn't exist yet. When we approach Jobs's idea with a victor mindset, we start looking back and thinking, 'Ah, I get it now. I understand the process that got me here.' As victims, we find ourselves stuck in the game, looking for quick wins, missing opportunities. As victors, we can step back from the game, sit in the grandstand and see it unfold from an elevated vantage point. We can *enjoy* the game.

Ultimately, we have to acknowledge that what our inner voice is saying can manifest itself on the outside.

When we talk nicely to ourselves – when we give ourselves the time of day – we might just discover that there is some magic hidden in all of us.

Some people might talk of chi or karma, and when we consider the various esoteric sciences that are being explored – for example, the science around plant communication (yes, plants communicating) – it's hard to ignore the idea that unseen and unheard 'languages' can offer life-changing information. Some of these studies examine how fauna and flora can send airborne messages to one another as warning signals when reacting to pests and threats, encouraging them to grow faster or release defensive chemicals.

The acacia example: The giraffe's favourite food is the acacia tree and the average giraffe might mill around in the same spot eating acacias all day if he could. But he can't. Although giraffes have developed exceptionally long tongues and tough lips with which they can gingerly pluck delicious leaves from thorny acacia branches, the hardy trees have developed a natural defence mechanism to ward off the hungry herbivores. By releasing terrible-tasting tannins on sensing that it is under attack, the acacia deters the giraffe from stripping its foliage all in one go. More than that, the tree releases chemicals that tell its neighbouring acacias to start releasing *their* tannins before the giraffe even gets to them. Voila: the power of plant communication!

I'm not saying we must believe in the things we cannot see; I'm saying we need to take a moment to marvel at the magic that we often allow ourselves to easily dismiss – both around us and within.

There will always be someone calling 'bullshit' on everything (the internet will tell you as much), but we should choose to focus our attention on the magic – rather than only taking in what we have been taught and thus limiting our potential.

There's so much you can choose to believe in, so why not start by believing in yourself?

THE VICTOR'S SUMMARY

For great success – be it in work or play or life in general – you need to be a positive victor. You need to believe in yourself. If you don't, then it's time to change your mindset, and applying the 3Rs is the way to do it; in fact, it's the way to change anything in your life. The rewards throughout the process are astonishing.

My good friend and poet, Andrew Arnott, once told me that his intention was to get out of his head and into his heart. He said:

'My head is a swimming pool and my heart is the ocean.' This sums it up perfectly: when we get into the victor mindset the opportunities are not contained, they are endless.

CHAPTER FOUR

FOREVER PROFITABLE

Tracking our rapidly changing times and trends to prepare for the future

The ability to engage with the world with a victor mindset is the fire that fuels winning outcomes; I believe it is the necessary foundation for any individual, business or corporation to build sustained, genuine success. But let's be honest: we can't prosper purely on the merits of our good habits.

To create cutting-edge organisations that can thrive in our shifting business landscape, we will need to drink from the fountain of insight and look into the future of technology, industry, consumers and employees. How can we 'predict' the future and what does it take to remain, what I call, Forever Profitable?

The good news is that if you keep an eye on the world around you and **learn how to categorise and contextualise trends** you don't need to be an oracle to see what your future might look like: intelligent anticipation is preparation.

In my years of strategic consulting, I have become fascinated by the fact that so many organisations consistently battle with one essential aspect that the future inevitably demands: change. Companies are often so successful and good at doing what they've always done that the notion of changing the way they operate is prohibitively scary. But the idea that 'if it's not broken, don't fix it' only makes sense if you can understand and anticipate how it *might* be broken. And in today's world the ways in which things might be broken, and the likelihood of this happening, are increasing every day.

To address this fundamental oversight, I developed Forever Profitable, the methodology that I now apply to all my strategic and trend-consulting engagements. As markets, consumer needs and the world in general keep shifting, many businesses struggle to keep up with new and fluctuating trends and stay afloat – never mind profitable. As we've seen, I can relate to this reluctance to change patterns because I too used to be narrow-minded and dogmatic about the way I ran my businesses. And, yes, it worked out for a while. But back then I had no idea how to innovate when confronted with change, and ultimately it cost me my livelihood.

I developed Forever Profitable because I came to realise that the way I had done business previously was based on a broken construct – one that was becoming increasingly outdated in the modern business world. I found that, whereas I had to look to my personal past to grow up as an individual, I had to look to the future to be able to operate effectively in business today.

But while trends are now my thing, I'll be the first to tell you that they are not all worth lusting after.

This chapter will show you how to dissect and apply relevant trends, how to fathom the terrain of your business landscape, and how to implement sustainable strategies.

Now is a good time to start thinking about your major goal – your Moonshot – because we are about to find out how to get there. I'm going to share the thinking process and the steps that I follow in real-world scenarios because I believe that anyone can, and should, apply the Forever Profitable methodology, whether you run a small business or a global corporation. When you do create your Moonshot at the end of the book, you will need to grasp the space that your Moonshot lives in and approach innovation with a victor mindset that offers you a clear picture of what it takes to stay ahead.

THE TRANSITION TO AN EXPONENTIAL FUTURE

Before we can actively engage in this process, we need to appreciate that we are in a transitional phase in modern human history and we need a foundational understanding of what it is that's driving the major change in business today – change that we're seeing all around us. Bear with me as I channel my inner history teacher for a few pages.

Energy, communication and transport are the foundations of Western capitalism as we know it today. As the likes of economic and social theorist Jeremy Rifkin have outlined, these are the critical factors that have influenced how global trade and business takes place.

If we look back to the 18th and 19th centuries, we see that the start of the first industrial revolution and the beginning of capitalism were fuelled by a new energy source: steam power (from coal). This was, in essence, the first form of widely used, accurately harnessed energy that didn't involve man or animal power. Steam power dramatically shaped industry of the time in two particularly important ways: the revolution of communication, thanks to the introduction of steam-powered printers; and the revolution of transport, which was accelerated by steam-powered locomotives and ships, expanding transport networks across the Western world and facilitating the swelling scales of production and commerce.

If we fast-track to the beginning of the 20th century, we see the effects of a second industrial revolution. In this transition the use of fossil fuels (coal, oil and natural gases) for energy became more feasible and effective, bringing with it fast-expanding and world-changing electrical grids. Likewise, the oil-powered combustion engine superseded steam power, and the efficiency of transport was transformed by planes, (electric) trains and automobiles; suddenly, we were able to move around a lot faster for a lot cheaper. Communication also advanced in great leaps as electricity became mainstream; now we could communicate across the world almost instantly (though not cheaply), and in time we gained access to radio, television and faster printers.

In this view, industrial glory reached its peak between 2000 and 2007, by which stage this second industrial revolution was as fast and efficient as it could be. It felt like the (Western) world was flush with cash as business boomed – but the visible cracks started to appear in 2008 with the start of the global financial meltdown.

Today we can see that we stand on the cusp of a new era, one in which fossil fuels are being replaced by renewable energies, communication (and culture) is being constantly and profoundly shaped by the influence of the internet, and transport is transforming under the influence of modern technology. While the communication transition is the most visible to us right now, both as individuals and in business, the other two are fast following suit.

Though the industrial world still relies heavily on fossil fuels, the movement towards renewables has begun and the pace with which we make the change will only increase. Solar power, in particular, has enormous potential; not only is it a 'clean' energy, but it is abundant and decentralised. The rapidly advancing technology of photovoltaic cells – along with wind turbines and other renewable technologies – will see this new energy becoming more accessible and increasingly affordable in the near future. (Similarly, nuclear energy appears to be on the cusp of a new technological revolution.)

Communication as we know it today has largely moved to the internet, which has also changed the way we expect communication to occur, the frequency at which it occurs, and the price we pay for it – which is effectively nothing.

When it comes to transport, the emergence of pilotless drones and driverless cars no longer seem like something from sci-fi movies; they are happening right now and they will only make transport more efficient. As more and more cars controlled by artificial intelligence appear on our roads, the reduction in traffic congestion and the resulting access to what was previously 'lost time' will have profound effects on our lives – never mind the profound safety benefits we will enjoy.

As examples of how energy, transport and communication are being revolutionised, consider:

 ENERGY: the Tesla Powerwall
Launched in 2015, the Tesla Powerwall offers the potential to change the way individuals and businesses generate and use electricity around the world. Essentially a rechargable lithium-ion battery, the Powerwall allows you to effectively store rooftop solar energy (or electricity from the grid when rates are low) for use at night or at peak requirement times, allowing you to significantly cut your grid-based energy consumption or even become completely energy independent. It can also be used as backup during power outages. How is this different from other battery-pack systems? At a cost of a few thousand dollars, depending on requirements, the tech has finally broached a point where we have relatively affordable access to enough storable energy for it to be practical and workable.

Which is to say, in the right market and conditions (depending on the grid cost of electricity and the abundance of solar energy), it will pay itself off over time – and it will get more viable as the technology improves. As an added bonus, Tesla has adopted from Apple the understanding that game-changing devices must be user-friendly and funkily futuristic looking, so that people actually want to use them.

 COMMUNICATION:
WhatsApp and similar apps
Not too long ago we interacted with friends and colleagues by phone and in person. Email and then video-conferencing (or Skype) were part of the first disruptive revolution, and now WhatsApp (incorporated in 2009 – barely the other day) and similar smartphone apps have advanced things even further. The use of WhatsApp has reduced communication costs to practically zero, making interactions instant and considerably easier. As a result, communication has proliferated: as of early 2016, more than a billion WhatsApp users around the world were sending 42 billion messages a day. Many apps now have this type of free communication accessibility built in so that, whether you're rating your Uber driver or updating your exercise activity to your medical insurer, there are means and metrics for companies and customers to interact with each other on an ongoing basis.

TRANSPORT: driverless Ubers

Uber - publically launched in San Francisco in 2011 - is the yardstick example of today's disruptive business (one we'll return to regularly). From a personal perspective, taking a taxi to the airport used to cost me 40 percent more before I started using Uber. But when driverless (electric) Uber cars are introduced this price will continue to decrease. And if the trip is optimised when several passengers are travelling the same route, the price will be reduced once again.

So we can see that things aren't just 'speeding up' or 'becoming more efficient'; we are in the midst off a profound change in modern industry, which is affecting the way people interact and do business. I like to think that we used to live in a linear world where taking ten steps forward meant moving ten metres ahead – that was logical and made sense. But modern technology, powered by computational speeds that double on a regular basis, has led us to a tipping point after which quantum leaps have become the norm.

Today business, and society in general, is engaged in a symbiotic relationship with modern technology, and as a result we are seeing exponential progressions everywhere.

This means that we are moving towards a future that allows us to make massive strides as opposed to incremental micro-steps. Now taking ten steps forward may mean you're a thousand metres ahead – or perhaps you're in a different place altogether.

We've only just begun this trajectory and it's still early days, but by 2020 we have to be prepared to think about the effects of exponential growth on both a personal and a business level. If we take just one example, namely the rapid advancements in 3D printing, how will our lives as we know it change when we start 3D printing our own knives and forks? How will manufacturing be affected, considering that brands like New Balance, Adidas and Nike are already exploring the prospects of custom, on-demand 3D shoe printing? Now that 3D printed pills are also a reality, how will our health and wellness be affected when we can wake up to a customised tablet that can be produced on the spot, catering for our daily mineral and vitamin deficiencies?

How will we remain profitable (and sane) in a brave new world that's so different to the world we thought we knew?

The future will be a very different animal and the world ahead won't look anything like the world behind us. We might be very good at reviewing the history of our business and extrapolating success tactics, but this supposedly logical move won't work if the future is an entirely new creature. Looking into the rear-view mirror is becoming increasingly irrelevant in the face of exponential growth.

A business used to stay profitable by keeping the proverbial ship afloat, keeping operations on track and services consistent – this used to almost guarantee success. Now, in order to remain profitable, we have to be asking brand-new questions, in particular: how do we rapidly and continuously innovate and how can we create a future-forward company culture? As a result, in the United States, the role of a Chief Future Officer (or Head of Innovation) is fast becoming an integral part of the business decision-making group; a voice of reason that drives evolution based on what is coming, rather than what has been.

THE SIX Ds

There are going to be seven billion people on the internet by 2023.

This means: more access to information and knowledge, more connectivity, and more digitisation. But this growth isn't going to magically become a fact on the 1st of January 2023 – it is happening right now at an exponential rate and it is laying down the gauntlet for us to change.

Much of my thinking is inspired by the visionary entrepreneur, speaker and author Peter Diamandis, who is also co-founder of the Singularity University (SU). Based in Silicon Valley, SU aims 'to educate, inspire, and empower leaders to apply exponential technologies to address humanity's grand challenges'.

Together with Steven Kotler, Diamandis has co-authored two books, *Abundance* and *Bold*; both are excellent resources, and the latter reflects on much of what SU stands for and aims to impart. To explain the process of exponential growth and the clear pattern that emerges, I have used Diamandis and Kotler's 'The Six Ds' of exponential organisations to outline the steps that lead to disruption. Although I have changed the order of the six Ds, the contributing factors remain the same, namely: Digitisation, Deceptive Growth, Dematerialisation, Demonetisation, Democratisation and Disruption.

1 **Digitisation** is the beginning point from which products and services eventually become free or virtually free. The moment something is digitised – be that a product or a service – the rest of the Ds are bound to follow.

Cameras are the perfect example of a product that was digitised. Not only did digital cameras replace the previous technology (film cameras), but the standalone camera itself has largely been replaced, incorporated into one of the most disruptive devices in history, the smartphone.

2 **Deceptive Growth** occurs after something becomes digitised. It may look like it won't happen at first, but then it starts expanding steadily, gaining traction and then doubling in growth on a regular basis, leading to exponential strides.

The resolution of the first digital cameras in the mid-1970s, for instance, was around 0.01 megapixels, hopelessly inadequate for practical photography. But as this doubled and eventually reached 1 megapixel, the exponential growth from 1 to 2 and then to 4 megapixels happened almost in the blink of an eye – suddenly digital cameras weren't just viable, they were the obvious choice.

3 **Dematerialisation** occurs as a result of digitisation and deceptive growth. It means that the industry is taken from a physical format into a digital space.

General media – music, film, books, newspapers and, of course, photography – are the obvious examples.

4 **Demonetisation** happens when products and services become free or virtually free. When something is dematerialised it becomes replicable at no cost.

For example, a photograph posted on Facebook or a video uploaded on YouTube can be downloaded and 'consumed' millions of times at no apparent cost.

5 **Democratisation** means that everyone can have access to it. This has become true for education, photography, news reporting, music and movies – with more to come.

The likes of video rental giant Blockbuster and any number of print media companies have been obliterated since people stopped paying for democratised products. At the same time, anyone can become a photographer, musician or filmmaker as the tools to produce and distribute media have become democratised.

6 **Disruption** is the end result that changes the way an industry works. Disruption inevitably sees the rise to prominence of new winners and the consignment to history of the losers who failed to adapt and thus remain profitable.

In the camera industry, compare the success of 2002 startup GoPro to the decline of Kodak, once *the* photography brand, which filed for bankruptcy in the US in 2012.

If we agree that Digitisation is affecting most industries, then we can foresee the end result:

DISRUPTION

In essence, our very understanding of the capitalist model we thought we knew is changing, as so many aspects of the modern economy become more efficient and less expensive, and as the previously centralised system becomes ever more decentralised.

The critical understanding, then, as we head towards the 'sharing economy', is the need to tap into trends to understand the need-shifts in markets, technologies, industries, consumers and employees. If we want to make profitable changes, we need to understand the lifecycle of innovation and how it can lead to the final 'D': *disruption*.

The Forever Profitable methodology is designed to help organisations focus on building an innovative and change-driven strategy that is both implementable and sustainable in a future where disruption is the name of the endgame.

FOREVER PROFITABLE
IN 3 STEPS

There are three steps to the Forever Profitable process. By going through each step, you can create a future-focused roadmap.

STEP 1: Evaluate the future of technology, your industry, your consumer and your employee
STEP 2: Introduce the Culture S.T.A.R.S and R.A.P.I.D. Innovation techniques
STEP 3: Implement gamification

The first two steps involve a process I call Trenovate, which is a way of categorising and contextualising trends in order to innovate with purpose.

On their own, trends are little more than good entertainment. You can find the most fascinating trends in just a few minutes on the internet, and they are likely to lead you down a rabbit hole in which you will come face to face with the exponential coming of the future – which can be exciting and daunting at the same time.

You could, for instance, quite easily lose yourself in the allure of the 'Emotionology' trend: how emotions and moods can be monitored or altered through technology with wearable devices such as Thync. But unless you are in the business of psychology, medicine or pharmaceuticals, this trend may not be worth your time and effort.

The way I like to look at trends is with the intention of innovating a specific business. When trends are combined with innovation and purpose, wonderful things can happen.

To streamline the process of uncovering relevant trends, we must delve into examining what I call the 'Four Pillars' on which an economy – and therefore a business – is reliant: the future of technology, your industry, your consumer and your employee. When trends are categorised and contextualised into these pillars, they become more than just entertainment: they become tools that guide us towards the future, enabling laser-focused innovation to occur.

STEP 1
Evaluating the future of technology, your industry, your consumer & your employee

The Four Pillars that affect an organisation are changing rapidly in these exponential times, and it's up to us to identify how they keep moving an economy forward; how they drive exponential shift and change, and how it drives them. As we've seen, we are currently in the midst of a transition in modern human industry; we are witnessing a reinvention of capitalism and an emergence of the sharing (or hybrid) economy.

Peer-to-peer sharing of resources, on-demand services and collaborative ventures are only the tip of the sharing-economy iceberg.

Most companies are thoroughly versed in one of the four pillars: the future of their industry. But in my experience their underestimation of technology leaves them vulnerable to tech-enabled potential disruptors, and they tend not to understand the future of their consumer and employee needs very well. For success in the longer game, strategic business decisions that are based on an understanding of only one of the pillars just aren't good enough. You need to embrace all of them.

By creating a roadmap for your business using the Four Pillars, you can start evaluating your future needs based on the real trends that are emerging. Regular analysis of the pillars will then offer you a holistic approach to making business decisions.

Pillar 1: The Future Of Technology

In the linear growth world of yesteryear, the information technology (IT) and digital/technology departments used to be small (or non-existent) components of an organisation. IT generally used to begin and end with the stereotypical 'computer guy' who managed internal office networks or would be on call to check if a computer was plugged in when it didn't work. It was a small business unit that wasn't a high priority in operations, strategy and marketing.

These days, technology has become ubiquitous and intertwined with almost every aspect of our lives and businesses, from the way we measure how long we brush our teeth ('There's an app for that') to the way we order a taxi or a pizza or a massage, to the way we interact with our customers and clients. The IT and digital/technology departments of almost every organisation, specifically leading ones, no longer sit in the background; they are integral to success. 'Digital-first' and 'mobile-first' are buzzwords that stem from technology's ability to disrupt us, disrupt our competitors and create brand-new platforms.

Getting to grips with the 'Future of Technology' pillar is essential in the Trenovate process and requires us to focus on how tech makes consumers' lives more seamless and employees' lives more fluid.

Understanding the future of technology is imperative for us to anticipate the disruptor that a competitor might be creating for us so that we can create it first – and disrupt ourselves and them in the process. If we're ready for it, we can allow the disruption to work for us.

Perhaps most importantly, technology can deeply affect companies by entirely replacing core management and operational structures that used to be essential. In 2016 the Momentum Machines startup in San Francisco announced it would open a robot-run burger joint – that may seem like a novel concept now, but how long do we have until technology and robotics replacing management and staff become the norm in the service industry?

Similarly, banking and FinTech are at the forefront of using tech as a disruptor. Consider the enormous time saving that came with the introduction of online banking two decades ago. Suddenly you didn't have to stand in a queue to make a deposit. That was revolutionary then, but today we're seeing entirely new platforms like thelendingclub.com that bypass banks entirely and allow you to borrow from peers. If banking is your industry, this is the tech you need to be investigating: ideas that seemed crazy yesterday but which may sink your business tomorrow.

Elsewhere, technology reveals our exponential future wherever we turn. It seems we were swearing at our dial-up modems just the other day, but now tech is becoming more and more ingrained into our everyday reality: we – and our clients and customers – are permanently connected if we choose to be.

The Jacquard example: A Levi's and Google collaboration is just one good example of the leaps and bounds we are seeing in technological development: called 'Project Jacquard', it is pioneering the concept of wearable technology by weaving conductive yarns into the clothes we wear, yielding textiles that can perform as touch and gesture surfaces. (If you're interested you may want to... Google it.)

Technology has become so decisive that it often seems that for any modern brand to survive it must become a technology brand in one way or another. This is particularly true for the hugely influential car brands, which are partnering with tech giants to advance self-driving intelligence and device connectivity to collect and deliver data. Hyundai, for example, has partnered with design firm IDEO to include multi-sensory mood-enhancing features. Similarly, Mercedes-Benz has plans to create a car that responds to your state of health by using the steering wheel to monitor heart rate, auto-adjusting ambient temperature, sound and lighting to improve driver comfort and wellbeing.

The next step will be to physically embed technology into our bodies so that we can make better use of it. Yes, we are destined to become cyborgs. Apple's Airpods, the first mainstream version of semi-embedded devices, are a tentative step in this direction.

The tech evolution is here to stay and its ability to worm its way into every crevice of our lives multiplies its significance.

Of all the pillars, this is the one you need to keep your eyes on at all times because it has the most potential for quick, game-changing disruption.

Pillar 2: The Future Of Your Consumer

Henry Ford once said that if he had asked his consumers what they wanted they would have told him, 'A faster horse.' He gave them the model-T Ford, the world's first affordable car. Steve Jobs similarly judged that his customers would never have asked for an iPod; they would have requested a five-disc Discman – that's a portable CD player for those readers who were never exposed to this ancient technology.

The lesson is thus an old one that remains as relevant today as it's ever been. We need to distance ourselves from what our consumers say they want (or think they want) because the truth is: they don't have all the answers. Running costly focus groups and pleading with customers to tell us what they want is not always the best idea, because they themselves might not know what they need until they have it.

To succeed, we must give our consumers what they want before they know what that is – and, to do that, we must understand our consumers' needs better than they do.

All business involves some form of communication, and to connect with our consumers – no matter whether we're an Apple-type corporation or a small, family-run business – we need to know who we are speaking to and what 'language' they speak. Working with the trends that move our consumers allows us to innovate and become more attractive to our target market by pre-empting their needs rather than asking them what they need. When you understand your consumers' needs, you are able to pinpoint the language you need to use and you can build your business around their specific requirements.

The 5 Need States

In order to adapt to the changing business landscape we need to understand trends, and to understand trends we need to grasp the changing human needs that drive them. If we are able to dissect trends and understand the changing dynamics of human needs, we can, to some extent, predict the future.

The term 'need states' refers to the differing human needs that are affected by the digitisation of the world around us. People with different need states have different expectations of how the brands they interact with should treat them as consumers and employees. As modern consumers, we have developed a type of ambient intelligence around the experiences that we seek; how we are understood and how we want to live our lives. Anything that is digital has an inherent ability to measure, track and personalise things for us, and as a result we are becoming more spoiled and more focused on brands that can feed our need states.

The five need states to look out for now are:
- Hyper-Personalisation
- Hyper-Convenience
- Hyper-Trust
- Hyper-Recognition
- Hyper-Value

These are the five driving forces behind most current trends, and if you assess any business that is tuning into one or more of them, you'll likely find that they are interpreting the relevant trends well. To illustrate them we need only look at the benchmark example of a modern disruptive company, Uber, which has honed in on four of the five needs.

Uber hasn't really changed the concept of taxis, but it has changed the way we access them because it has been able to deliver a platform and service that is directly in line with consumer needs.

- It is hyper-personalised: you control the app, which knows your preferences.
- It is hyper-convenient: it's easy to use, you can order a taxi quickly, and you can track your car's progress almost to the second.
- It is hyper-trustworthy: it has systematically built a global reputation based on smart publicity and quick and helpful customer feedback.

■ It is hyper-valuable: getting an Uber is already much cheaper than ordering a regular taxi, and it is likely to get cheaper.

Customers, consumers, users, target audience – call them what you will, the people in your market have at least one of these five hyper-needs.

The pizza examples: The world of international-brand pizza delivery is exceptionally trend aware. For example, Domino's Pizza in the US and elsewhere has created a zero-click app that has refined the hyper-convenience need to the finest possible degree. On downloading the app, users fill in their credit card details, location and favourite pizza order, and thereafter ordering a pizza is as easy as opening the app. Once opened, a ten-second timer starts; if the user doesn't make any changes in that time their favourite order will be paid for and delivered.

If you think that's radical, consider 'the world's first pizza-ordering tattoo', introduced by Pizza Hut in the UK. Using QR technology, customers can simply scan a nifty, pizza-shaped temporary tattoo with their smartphone to have their favourite order delivered to their location. In this instance, the gimmick element provides potential for publicity, boosting brand recognition, while the hyper-convenient and hyper-personalisation need states are validated.

By focusing on specific consumer needs, Domino's and Pizza Hut have been able to interpret relevant trends in their markets and create unique experiences for their customers.

I would say they have Trenovated the way pizzas are ordered.

The 3 Markets

There is more research on markets and consumers across the planet than you have time to read in a lifetime, so for our purposes we will focus on the three overarching markets we are likely to cater for: the mature awareness market, the emerging market and the less-affluent market.

THE MATURE AWARENESS MARKET

The mature awareness market can be found in cosmopolitan and highly developed cities such as San Francisco, Sydney, Berlin and pockets of Cape Town.

This market is underpinned by a mega-trend called 'guilt-free consumption', which drives conscious behaviour affecting the way people eat, what they buy (anything from clothing to real estate to consumables) and how they use transport.

It shapes the way people interact with the world and encourages them to ask, 'What impact am I having on my surroundings and the world in general, and how can I lessen my footprint?'

The need states for the mature awareness market include: **hyper-personalisation**, **hyper-convenience** and **hyper-trust**; needs that delivered the sharing economy and have brought about the development of companies like Airbnb.

The mature awareness market also made it cool to ride bicycles to work, grow vegetables in back gardens or on rooftops and share all of this and more on Instagram. Instead of buying into fast-fashion, this market prefers the idea of 'normcore fashion', which is about wearing basic clothes that let you blend into a multitude of different groups more easily. If the clothes have been ethically produced and sourced, all the better.

Understanding what drives this market will help you to tap into the language, services and products that speak to this consumer. Mature awareness consumers are highly informed and sensitive to brands that are trying to bullshit their buyers: they don't like to be fooled and when they find out they have been, business tends to suffer.

The sweatshop example

In 2000, *The Guardian* in the UK exposed allegations that popular sport brand Adidas had been supplied by Indonesian factories that underpaid and overworked minors in 'barbaric' conditions. It was one of many such 'sweatshop' allegations related to any number of global apparel brands at the time, and closely followed the publication of Naomi Klein's game-changing book *No Logo*. Today, the likes of Adidas, Nike and H&M are acutely aware of their eagle-eyed target consumers, which has pushed them to become more accountable in their manufacturing processes, whether directly or indirectly responsible. Promoting fair working conditions – by collaborating with non-profit organisations, conducting transparent audits and implementing strict working and contractual policies – isn't just the ethically correct thing to do; it's an actively positive brand attribute.

The world's most influential and affluent folk are concentrated in mature awareness markets, but they don't always flaunt their wealth and the way they spend their vast sums of money is not always as you'd have expected in the past. This is most acutely noticeable in the growing movement for billionaires to give the bulk of their money away through initiatives such as The Giving Pledge (givingpledge.org), and it is an indication that, in the sharing economy, wealth is becoming more about experience and access as opposed to ownership.

THE EMERGING AWARENESS MARKET

This market can be found in cities such as Dubai, Beijing, Johannesburg, Miami and Kuala Lumpur.

The motto here is: bigger, better, faster. The people in this market are heavily influenced by the 'conspicuous consumption' mega-trend and are literally emerging within the economic power houses that their cities are becoming.

It's not hard to see why displaying status is important to these consumers: just a generation ago Dubai was still considered little more than a desert wasteland, Beijing was barely emerging from the constrains of China's communist strictures, and Johannesburg was segregated by apartheid. Now the middle class is booming in these cities and their emerging markets are flourishing.

When you visit any one of these cities you can see how emerging wealth has shaped the type of world that has been built: there are shopping centres on every block and blinged-up supercars at every turn. Luxury brands like Louis Vuitton and Gucci, which focused almost exclusively on the mature awareness market two decades ago, are operating in these regions for the first time and taking full advantage of consumers who previously missed out and are now ready to spend spend spend. This is a world apart from what is happening in the mature awareness market, where brands such as Hugo Boss are closing physical stores, branded luxury clothing is not performing as well as it used to, and online clothing sales are steadily increasing.

It's no surprise, then, that **hyper-personalisation** and **hyper-recognition** are major need states in emerging awareness markets. This is why you'll find expensive cars parked outside houses that cost less than the cars and selfie sticks that are never far from reach. When these consumers are shopping for your brand, feeding the recognition they require offers ego-boosting opportunities as they let the world know they have splurged.

The need for recognition is not limited to buying products; the services offered in these markets need to be fit for royalty, and customers and clients are often off-kilter when making requests.

A personal example: When I was running my restaurants in Johannesburg – as opposed to Cape Town and Pretoria – the level of expectation for good service often bordered on the ludicrous. Certain customers wanted to be treated like kings and queens and were often quite crude about their demands. It wasn't only that they wanted the menu changed, or even called for ingredients that weren't on the menu at all, it was also that the demands were being delivered with the rudeness of a spoilt child. Even when it came to gratuities, they would often only leave a generous tip if other people were looking. My waiters frequently complained about these thrifty diners who would eat lamb chops and drink Champagne but watch their pennies when the bill arrived. In my service industry experience, customers with 'new money' tend to have an immature approach to how they want to receive service, whereas customers from the mature awareness market tend to be kinder and have more realistic expectations (though that doesn't guarantee a good tip!).

In South Africa alone we have millions of people who comfortably fit into the emerging awareness market bracket, and brands that are talking to them need to understand that they've got money, it's disposable and they want to spend it – often spending more than they have. It's a very profitable market to get into, but companies need to dance to their tune and fulfil their needs at every turn.

THE LESS-AFFLUENT MARKET

This market is, broadly speaking, located in the townships of every Third World city and the low-income neighbourhoods of every First World city across the globe.

Its consumers are driven by a key desire to get out of the less-affluent market and into the emerging market, where they can afford to wear brand-name clothes and drive top-marque cars. Less-affluent markets are motivated by the value-driven consumption mega-trend.

These consumers prioritise immediate needs and worry how far they can stretch their buck. Need states include **hyper-value**, most notably, but also **hyper-convenience** and **hyper-recognition**. They buy in small quantities on a daily basis and don't plan beyond the week ahead because their money usually won't last that long.

There are two notable trends that tie into this market's needs. The first is 'reverse innovation', which drives people to innovate out of necessity and create (often unbelievably) cheap, efficient solutions that emulate what can be achieved in the mature and emerging markets.

The car examples: In 2008 Tata Motors announced their plans for a $1,000 car, the 'cheapest car in the world', which would allow customers in less-affluent markets, particularly India, to trade in their scooters for a low-cost car that would give them a sense of being in the emerging market. Initial demand was so strong that there were 200,000 orders before the first model rolled off the assembly line.

But reverse innovation is often evident on a smaller, more personal scale. A few years ago, I came across a resourceful man in Langa township, Cape Town, who was using washing machine parts to fix cars. This may be a low-cost and less effective solution than a formal mechanic, but the *need* was so strong that it drove the potential to create opportunities – which is to say, the man had customers.

Connectivity is the second essential trend that can present a way to move out of the less-affluent and into the emerging market. In early 2014 MTN, one of the major telecoms providers in Africa, innovated with this understanding in mind by launching their

'MTN Internet Bus' in Uganda, offering commuters free, high-speed Wi-Fi coverage and access to sixteen high-end computer workstations.

Similarly, Kenyan tech startup Mawingu Networks has set up internet hotspots in rural villages by using a combination of solar power, TV white space and microwaves to establish Wi-Fi networks. These examples are testament to future-conscious innovations that have been spawned from this market's trends and needs.

The consumers in each of the three markets can sometimes have similar needs but very different underpinning mega-trends affecting them, and the business model I'm outlining in these pages relies on an understanding of these trends, which can be filtered down into finer detail. Depending on your business and goals, it might be useful to recruit market research experts who can unearth the different layers and nuances of a specific market.

With that in mind, ask yourself some questions.

1 Which market(s) are you targeting?
2 What are your consumers' needs?
3 What mega-trends are they following?
4 In our crazy new world, how can you channel these answers into being Forever Profitable?

Identifying the changing needs of consumers

As markets change, needs change too. Your task is to keep exploring what motivates your market. Needs and motivators can vary depending on how much time a consumer has had money for, what their awareness is like and how much they have matured emotionally.

From my own perspective, when I lived in Johannesburg in my late twenties my primary motivating need was to make money and spend it on flashy things to show off. Today, living in Cape Town, I am a minimalist, at the other end of the scale: the coolest thing I can do right now – my way of showing off – is *not* buy flashy things and *not* show off.

Forecasting the future of your consumer means getting in touch with the motivating factors that allow people to show up and express what their idea of success is. In so doing, you will redesign your business to meet new needs by continuously evaluating your product, service, packaging, technology, and social and environmental impact.

Creating the right customer journey

The 'right' customer journey places the needs first at every turn:

1 What are you selling? And does it consider your consumers' needs?

2 Can consumers relate to the service you provide?
3 Does the packaging speak to your consumers?
4 What is the complete experience?
5 Does technology create a more seamless process?
6 What is the social and environmental impact?

Don't underestimate how needy your consumers really are. When you look at each point of the journey, you must be able to thoroughly address the needs of the market you are aiming at.

For example, a mature awareness consumer wants a product that is served in a seamless and calm way, with minimal or sustainable packaging, providing a personalised experience with ambient intelligence and delivering tech that runs quietly in the background and with an ethical social and environmental impact.

The emerging market consumer wants a much bigger, brighter, bolder product and service that can be bombastic at times. Buying a flashy, loud and brash supercar is not the most environmentally friendly transport choice, but sustainable consumption is not necessarily a priority for emerging market consumers who are focused on living a life that was not previously available to them. The growth of international luxury brands – who may or may not practise conscious sourcing – in this market is also indicative of consumers' priorities. It's far more important that products and services make consumers the star of the show and enable them to use digital platforms as a means to publicly flaunt their purchases.

The Future Of Your Consumer is a pillar that you should be constantly revisiting and is critical to understand properly when creating products and services. Your consumer – that is, your target market – is not just a static profile: he or she is a shapeshifting person who is hyper-informed, has real needs and is hungry for innovation on all levels.

Pillar 3: The Future Of Your Industry

Here's the new reality: the future of your industry may well be reinvented by a sixteen-year-old kid in a pair of pyjamas.

Or it may be disrupted by a company that isn't even in your industry right now, but will be jumping into it soon with the intention of making your sector and your service irrelevant. Just look at what Napster and then Apple's iPod and iTunes did to the music industry: they made music stores irrelevant. In the blink of an eye, major CD manufacturers and megastores were no longer competing with one another and with companies in their industry; they were up against the technology that was wiping out the platform and the medium that they were using to make profit.

We have to understand the future of our industries because once we get a glimpse of who our possible disruptors could be, we need to either become them, buy them or copy them – and then morph our business into what it must look like in the future to thrive. Most likely, this will entail finding our feet in unfamiliar industries and creating new business offsprings in order to compete and stay relevant.

To predict the future of your industry or possible competitors, you need to establish which trends are affecting you and consider who the possible disruptors inside or outside of your industry may be.

If we take clothing as an example, what is happening in the clothing and fashion industries for our three broad markets? An upmarket brand like Patagonia (see p153) would be focused on the interests around conscious fashion and why this is important to their mature awareness market. Brands like H&M would need to consider the impacts of fast fashion on their emerging awareness market. And for their less-affluent market, a brand like PEP might explore survivor or value fashion trends.

You can employ professional market analysts to do this research or you can get hands on and do it yourself: read books, buy published research papers, trawl trend websites or simply ask your old friend Google.

Thinking like a disruptor

Most of the time disruptors arrive, apparently out of the blue, from another sector. Uber, for example, isn't another taxi business; it is a tech business. Taxi companies weren't even thinking about a player like Uber as their competitor until it came along and completely changed the very foundation of the taxi industry: how it works and how it caters to the need states of the market. Uber simply saw the changing needs before anyone else did – before anyone had even looked their way.

Disruptors are people or groups who understand the needs of their consumers and approach these needs without an emotional link or pre-set business model that must be followed.

Being overly attached to what you do – even if you do it really well – comes with the danger of overlooking change.

When we get overly caught up in the service or product we deliver, we can be disrupted. You might say that modern business is not about products or services any more; it's about solutions.

The Kodak example: The once dominant photography brand Kodak is an example of a business that was too attached to what it considered its operational strength to foresee and preempt the future of its industry – even though it came up with the disruptive technology that would sink it. The company claimed to be capturing 'Kodak moments', but it ignored the digital camera that one of its very own engineers had developed, because it was too focused on the photo-printing side of the business.

To identify a disruptor, you need to think like one.

A smart way to do this is to hire a small group of people whose only task is to get to grips with the need states in your market (see from p128) and then figure out how to disrupt your own business. It might sound a bit like shooting yourself in the foot, but either you do it in a controlled and manageable way or someone else will do it for you in a far more stressful manner.

For a medium-sized company that employs 50-200 people, an ideal team, in my opinion, would be five strong. Four members would be new or almost new to the industry and at least one would be a digital expert able to consider digital innovation. The appointed disruptors should not be immersed in the company or mingle in your office.

In looking for industry shifts and the resulting potential disruptions, you need to look at both international and local threats/opportunities. Understanding your immediate and local market is of course necessary, but the global village is real and only getting smaller; you need to figure out what is going on globally and foresee how this can be, might be, or will be applied locally.

For inspiration, just think Airbnb, Uber and any number of social media-related disruptors.

Convenience also plays a major role. How can you deliver in a new way? Who can you partner with to make your product or service more convenient? Maybe you need to diversify to cater for this new need. How can tech and automation help you personalise your business without requiring huge costs and more manpower? If the tech you need already exists, how can you integrate solutions that will take your current solution or workflow to the next level?

Predicting industry disruption

The companies I work with often struggle with this process of predicting disruption, which is fair enough given that disruptors often seem to come out of nowhere.

Remember the Domino's zero-click app (on p130)? Why has it disrupted other pizza brands? Not because Domino's pizza is the best in the world, but because their app speaks to the heart of what consumers are looking for – what they *need*. It's easy (convenient) and personalised (knows which pizza you like and where you are). Just like Uber, they didn't invent (or even reinvent) the wheel; they innovated how we access a service.

There are no clairvoyants who can truly predict how an industry will evolve, but we can begin to accept that **an industry will always be disrupted by someone who focuses on needs-serving solutions** – someone who understands the needs of our consumers better than we do. That's all it takes.

Finding future competitors

'Look at what your competition is doing' is old business wisdom to keep you looking over your shoulder – and I think it's becoming increasingly irrelevant. Of course you need to stay in the loop, but you must realise the limitations and even pitfalls at the same time.

Who's to say that your closest rivals today know exactly what's happening, or that they're looking in the right direction? If they're doing better than you, maybe this has to do with pricing or maybe a little luck's gone their way. Perhaps *you* actually have the chance to become the disruptor in your industry, but you're too distracted by your competitor's fabulous new Facebook campaign to realise it.

Future competitors won't be the same as your current competitors, so don't focus all your energy on what the adversaries are doing; broaden your horizons.

If you have been lucky enough to identify who your true competitors are and how these disruptors are going to make waves in your industry, you have a few choices.

1. You can steal or copy what they are doing and try to develop something similar;
2. You can partner with them – or synergise, if you prefer – to strategically deliver innovative solutions;
3. You can buy them out and branch out by allowing the new business unit to become a part of what you do.

When taking a closer look at the Future Of Your Industry pillar, the trickiest thing is to pinpoint who the competitor/disruptor is in the first place. Focusing on how your customers can access what you offer, rather than just the product or service itself, is also vital.

Remember, the needs should always come first.

Pillar 4: The Future Of Your Employee

In the United States, an estimated 50% of the workforce will be freelancing by 2020.

The trends emerging in the labour market are creating fundamental changes in the structure of organisations and the way they recruit and retain talent. If we want to build companies that are relevant in the eyes of our staff, we need to create ecosystems that are aligned with what this emerging specimen of worker desires.

Employees of the future are similar to entrepreneurs in the sense that they seek freedom (ability to work anywhere), flexibility (ability to work any time), autonomy (choice to work independently) and focused projects (freedom to commit to meaningful and varied work). These are the major drivers of this new, exciting employee type, and companies are taking full advantage because they want problem-solvers to work for them. That's what entrepreneurs who have to manage themselves do best: they see a problem and solve it because their business relies on this happening; they don't pass the buck.

Organisations are beginning to see the flaws in traditional hierarchical organisations, and to cater for the more autonomous future employee's needs they are seeking alternative management methods.

The self-management example: In the US, some boundary-pushing companies have started to adopt a radically different self-governing management method known as holacracy, 'a comprehensive practice for structuring, governing, and running an organization' that 'brings structure and discipline to a peer-to-peer workplace'.

In 2014 US-based online retailer Zappos – a regular on *Fortune's 100 Best Companies To Work For* list – embraced holacracy to the extent that it offered all staff a lucrative severance package in order to exit the company if they didn't want to accept the new management system. In an interview about the switch, CEO Tony Hsieh later wrote, 'Our march towards self-organization and self-management isn't an experiment. It's the future of work and it's the only structure that has stood the test of time [and] can become more innovative as it gets bigger (vs. typical corporate structures that become less innovative as they get bigger).'

Although holacracy has received criticism for being 'an operating system' that struggles to cater for irrational human emotion – with the result, for example, that team work could suffer – Zappos continues to embrace it, seeing benefits in the form of heightened creativity, trust and freedom. It may not be perfect yet, but employee self-management is destined to be on the future horizon as virtual organisations come to the fore.

This type of dispersed authority bodes well for budding contingent workers or entrepreneurs, and a business of the future can't afford to overlook how it will change the landscape of the workplace, job roles and management structures.

The employee of the future will actively seek out these new standards, and it is up to businesses to do what it takes to attract the staff of the future.

So who is this elusive cat we call the 'employee of the future'?

Getting to know the employee of the future

Identifying the 'why' that drives people is important not only for consumers, but also when attracting the right employees. Employees are consumers both inside and outside of a business. If we can create an authentic and sincere brand environment, this isn't just good for consumers; it's also good for attracting employees with a value system that suits our own.

The surfing example: Patagonia, an outdoor clothing and gear company established in Ventura, California in 1973, is a brand – a favourite of mine – that sincerely believes in the benefits of employing people who reflect its values. Patagonia is a certified B Corp company, the business equivalent of being a Fair Trade producer, or what I would call a 'conscious capitalist'; so you won't be surprised to learn that its focus is on the mature awareness market. Its CEO, Yvon Chouinard, is the author of *Let Them Go Surfing,* based on the idea that employees are happiest when they have some sort of freedom and can 'make a living without losing [their] soul'. Chouinard relishes the times when the office is empty because there is good surf and his employees are out there enjoying it. They may end up working less conventional hours but, according to this line of thinking, having the freedom and independence to enjoy things when the surf's up encourages and attracts people with the same value system as the Patagonia brand.

Although the label changes, the need states of employees and consumers remain very similar. It helps to think of employees as hyper-informed consumers who know a lot about the brand they support – its history, brand projection and values.

Modern employees are hyper-sensitive to the culture that they work in, the leadership style that manages them and the extent to which an organisation's values match their own.

I saw a job post recently that said 'Dog Lovers Only Apply' – and, whether they consciously know it or not, that is the company's value system. I could relate to it because, being a dog lover, I know what it's like when someone else shares this emotion and disposition – it speaks to my own values. When you have pre-existing and shared values in place, the link between the company and employee is already made to an extent.

Employees of the future want to know why companies do and believe what they do. Now that there is more transparency and emphasis around company culture, the questions asked by employees are much deeper and more meaningful than in the past. Organisations have to be mindful of the idea that they are managing hyper-sensitive employees who know their rights and compare value systems, directives and motivating factors.

To understand the future employee, it pays to look at the different generations and how needs can vary depending on age groups.

We can thank Millennials, a.k.a. Generation Y, for turning the traditional corporate machine on its head. These young guns came into the workplace asking new questions about why they had to be at work at a certain time, why they had to dress a certain way and why they needed to listen to the boss. Maybe everybody else was quietly asking the same questions before, but the Millennials had the guts to push for the change that is repositioning how we all work.

There is some contention around the exact dates and categories of worker 'generations', but popular opinion suggests the following:

Baby Boomers: born between World War II and the mid-1960s

Generation X: born between the mid-1960s and early 1980s

Generation Y / Millennials: born between the early 1980s and late 1990s

Generation Z: born between the mid-1990s and 2012
Alpha Generation: born after 2012

Currently, Generation Y makes up most of the workforce in the Western world. When they first entered the fray, the wise Baby Boomers and experienced Generation Xers would hear these newbies ask cheeky questions like, 'Can I work from home today?' or 'Can I wear shorts to the office?' Soon enough, the Baby Boomers and Generation Xers started having the same needs and thought, 'That's actually a pretty good idea…'

These questions brought about changes that have transformed the Baby Boomers, Generation X and Generation Y into what is known as 'Generation Flux' – the old needs merged with the new. Previous generations have had to un-learn the dogmatic, military style of management they once worked in, but now they are more flexible and have adopted a more democratic way of leading. At present, this leadership style is being driven towards new frontiers by the Millennials.

At the root of it all, motivations have shifted over time. Whereas Baby Boomers and Generation Xers coveted job security and might have miserably stayed in one company and one role for forty years, Millennials are more motivated by creativity than security. They are not blindly loyal and are harder to predict; when fed up or ready to move on, they will even resign before arranging another job.

Although needs and motivations determine career moves, an individual's market also affects their employee behaviour.

For example, Millennials in a less-affluent market may still regard job security as more of a priority, with emotional needs secondary.

Taking needs and market differences into consideration, we can categorise three types of employees:

1 People who seek a pleasurable life, always looking for the next party.

2 People who seek a secure life, with a white picket fence, steady job, happy family, and all the rest.

3 People – generally of the 'new' generation – who seek a meaningful life and want to use their skills for a greater cause.

Talent will future-proof a business.

Treating staff like partners attracts the brightest minds in the work force. This may mean implementing new management systems or styles that empower employees and give them the freedom to make meaningful decisions or to make an impact. For example, this can be achieved by creating small groups of no more than seven people who are tasked with solving short, focused problems, rather than being managed as part of a larger team that has less autonomy, clear direction and recognition.

Keep in mind that flexibility means employees now want to work from anywhere at anytime and might require the freedom to move in between companies and projects. On an emotional level, people want to share an organisation's vision and meaning. What can your company add that exceeds the purpose of working to make money?

Recruit and retain employees of the future.

Often clients say to me, 'You know, John, we have such rubbish staff. What can we do about it?' My answer to them is always, 'Ask yourself: where are your ideal employees working? The answer is: at the most lucrative, innovative and exciting companies.'

If your complaint is that you 'have rubbish staff', then the hard truth is that you might have a rubbish business or a rubbish business strategy, and people aren't excited about what you're doing. To attract the best people out there you need to develop a business model that's in line with where the world is going, then develop an innovative culture that can produce leaders and superstars based on the value system you have created.

The world's best companies have the best staff.

Once you've decided what sort of company you're going to be and are able to offer a future-forward workplace, staff will be attracted because you have created an environment that is aligned with their approach to living. The best perk for this new 'meaningful' person is value-driven, and not-money driven. To quote Simone Sinek:

'Those who believe what we believe offer their blood, sweat and tears. Those who don't believe what we believe demand more money or glory.'

Introducing the workplace of the future.

Digital platforms are the office space of the future. WordPress (operated by Automattic) provide a good example of this: they operate out of only one office space, in San Francisco, but they have a global workforce that interacts primarily via chat and meets at a project-driven conference once a year.

We're also seeing that modern businesses are setting up satellite offices in major capitals around the world, while employees in outlying areas can work from home, coffee shops, shared workspaces or anywhere with an internet connection. Quarterly or bi-annual team strategy meetings allow the global workforce to connect and then disperse again.

CLASSIFYING THE JOBS OF THE FUTURE

As we see that the nature of where and how we work is changing, we can see the potential for employees to become more nervous about how this affects their value within an organisation. So we need to consider, first, how the Millennial pursuit for autonomy may lead to redundancy and, second, how companies need to be prepared for the jobs of the future.

Can you imagine being replaced by a robot? You may think this a ridiculous notion, but a trend that has affected the blue-collar work force for decades – in the automation of factories, mines, warehouses and so on – is now making inroads elsewhere and we are all passive participants in the demise of job roles as we know them. We book our flights online, order a taxi with an app, and increasingly bypass the need for middle management.

Industries are being disrupted faster than ever before and past trends are no longer a reliable indicator of our future job prospects and the job roles as we know them now. Even such reputable careers as a doctor or financial advisor are at risk of being replaced by Artificial Intelligence (AI).

Don't panic.

Here's a quote from Pablo Picasso (from the 1960s) to put things in perspective: 'Computers are useless. They can only give you answers.' To me, this means that the jobs that harness emotional intelligence are where the future of (human) employment lies. With a clear focus on up-skilling for the (near) future, employees and companies can remain relevant.

Here is my list of ten jobs of the future:
1 **The rise and rise of the freelancer**
If freelancers are indeed the future of our workforce, employers need to create a flexible environment that will attract them and meet their needs. As we have seen, the traditional rules of work hours, dress code

and hierarchies are not for freelancers; they are driven by creativity, flexibility, freedom and autonomy.

2 'Solo' companies
If we become freelancers ourselves, our capacity and roles may vary, but in order for us to become a one-man or one-woman show we need to set up our personal brands just as a company would: with methodologies, marketing strategies and a brand identity.

3 Team organisers
Organisations will start hiring people with specific skills for short-term projects, which will require a human resources and management expert who knows how to find the right person to complement the team and its outcomes and then successfully run the team.

4 Urban farmers
Ever-growing populations and more awareness of how our food is produced are prompting the rise of urban farmers, who seek a healthier life and a more sustainable planet.

5 Longer-life planners
Medical innovations such as DNA sequencing and 3D bio-printing will allow us to become 'amortals' who defy the ageing process. This means we will

need to plan for living productive lives after reaching the current retirement age. As our average life-expectancy stretches ever upwards (notwithstanding the possibility of digitising our brains and thus living as long as we want...), we will see an increase in senior adults pursuing new ventures and ad-hoc work rather than hanging up their hats.

6 Senior caregivers

An ever-ageing population will require a new genre of caregivers. Although likely to be a combination of human and AI roles, this is a hugely growing sector.

7 Remote health-care specialists

Wearable tech and e-health sensors will be able to provide remote health practitioners with accurate information about symptoms and conditions.

8 Virtual reality designers

Virtual reality will soon be as normalised as our cellphones. The skills to build better virtual reality landscapes and experiences will be in hot demand.

9 3D print designers

As 3D printers become household items, we will be printing whatever we need ourselves, or at the local print shop. As this behaviour spreads so does the need for blueprint designers who can design anything from a mug or a spoon to, eventually, your house.

10 Ambient intelligence technicians

The combination of the Internet of Things (IoT), working from home and our need for hyper-convenience will require new specialist technicians who can, for example, link the carpet you step onto in the morning to the 3D printer in the kitchen that will produce your mineral tablet for the day in accordance with your level of nutritional requirements.

Your choice is simple: be scared of or be excited for the future. My advice is to take the victor's choice: get tooled up and find your new niche, because this exciting future is approaching at a dizzying speed.

Once you've identified your consumer's needs, you should examine your industry on a global and local level to figure out what's going on across all three markets. Then you need to hire the right employees to service the future of your consumer and industry. If you know how specific trends and need states apply to your market and to each of the Four Pillars that affect an organisation, you can start implementing innovative processes to secure your future.

STEP 2
Introducing new culture and innovation

The second step in the Forever Profitable methodology is the actual adoption and implementation of the roadmap. When I work with my clients, I do this by applying two programmes that I have created: what I call Culture S.T.A.R.S. and R.A.P.I.D. Innovation. By this point we will have categorised and contextualised relevant trends and are in a position to start preparing for the adoption of internal (Culture S.T.A.R.S.) and external (R.A.P.I.D. Innovation) trend-informed innovation – from developing employee rituals and culture to launching innovative change solutions.

Culture S.T.A.R.S.

We have already seen that employees don't want to be led by authoritarian management; they want innovation that will help them come into their own. The Culture S.T.A.R.S. methodology is designed to help individuals find success in their roles and is inspired by the way parents would encourage their children to follow their dreams and flourish, a concept that can also be applied in the workplace.

If your eight-year-old daughter came to you and said, 'I want to be a prima ballerina at the Royal Ballet when I grow up,' you might at first quiz her a little to find out where the motivation comes from. If it's serious (or even mildly serious at that age), you would make a commitment to one another in the shared belief that she could become a professional ballet dancer in time.

You would start realising that ambition by buying her a tutu and ballet shoes, enrolling her at the best ballet studio you can afford, and establishing appropriate new rituals: going to class regularly, taking her to see ballet performances, talking about ballet. You might also decorate her bedroom with ballerina motifs on the walls. Finally, you might encourage her to have a picture of her greatest ballet hero, whom she looks up to, on her bedside table so she can dream of becoming like her idol.

This is the type of process we might implement in our personal capacity at home in the hope that our loved ones will excel – yet you don't often encounter the same rules for achieving goals in the workplace. This is where Culture S.T.A.R.S. comes in (the acronym generally works in reverse order):

Story = the commitment you make together as parent and daughter
Rituals = changing your habits and behaviour in order to make her dream happen

Area = allowing your daughter's area or surroundings to reflect the story of her dream
Tools = making sure she is equipped with the right tools to be good at what she does
Staff (the Perfect Staff Member) = the perfect staff member to look up to (a prima ballerina in this case)

When following the S.T.A.R.S. method we can create an ecosystem that is based on the future of our business, because it allows people to believe in themselves and the shared commitment and thus succeed in their roles.

S = Story is the What-How-Why that defines your organisational values; your *raison d'être*. Your values are represented alongside this as actionable points that communicate where you need to get to, by when.

When you take into account the Four Pillars before shaping your story, you are able to really define your What-How-Why.

What are you going to be doing?

How are you going to do it?

Why are you doing it?

Then consider what values your staff need to have in order to attain the 'What?', and also what your timeline is for reaching your goals.

You should write no more than two sentences to describe your What-How-Why and Where-To-By-When. The language should be as simple as possible so that anybody can understand your values at a glance.

R = Rituals need to ingrain the Story into your culture. Just having a poster about your values up on a wall isn't enough. You need to ritualise your values into daily, weekly and monthly actions.

Rituals have the power to enforce values and performance; they can exist in various shapes and forms. Take the New Zealand All Blacks rugby team's Haka, for instance: it's a unique war dance (ritual) that is performed before every match. The ritual itself has absolutely nothing to do with rugby, but it has everything to do with invoking the warrior spirit in the players' energy and driving them to play better rugby.

These actions are the secret ingredient that can bring values to life within an organisation. As we've seen, to change behaviour, habits need to change – and to change habits, rituals need to be created.

However you choose to implement your rituals, they always need to support your story and your values.

Personal examples: Here are two examples of rituals that my team and I have helped conceptualise and implement for companies so that their employees could live their brand values.

1. For the South African whole foods and health products retailer Wellness Warehouse, we created a ritual based on their core values: 'fitness from inside-out'. The brand wanted their staff to portray the image of being fit and healthy, which resonates with the average profile of their customers.

We found that 70 percent of staff did not actually eat food from Wellness Warehouse because, first, the retail staff couldn't afford the produce and, second, food and drink like chia seeds and green tea are not part of the general South African eating culture. Our solution was to create a monthly ritual that involved staff participating in a five-kilometre team-building walk, at the end of which they all received vouchers to buy the food they wouldn't normally be able to afford. This ritual enhanced the value system around being healthy and fit, inside and out, and it allowed the staff to truly understand the products it was selling.

2. We created another ritual for an audio-visual (AV) company that included as one of its core values the line, 'Always be kiff' (cool). We considered where their staff weren't being 'kiff' and found that their technicians who set up massive events would end up rather smelly and grubby after an eight-hour shift involving some serious manual labour. As a result,

> by the time the guests started arriving, the AV staff
> looked far from 'kiff'. We responded by creating an
> 'Energy Ritual': we supplied a bag in each of the
> company vans containing a chocolate bar, an energy
> drink, hair gel, a new T-shirt and deodorant. Having
> finished setting up, the technicians could head back
> to the van, go through their energy ritual to freshen
> up and uphold the 'Always be kiff' value.

A = Areas and Artefacts in your business
environment need to reflect your Story. This covers
everything from your actual office space and interior
decor to your email signature, dress code and
equipment; all elements that make your staff feel
more in tune with your Story.

For instance, if your company Story is one that
focuses on fun or on health, you should have a fun
or healthy office space respectively to back this up.
It's about bringing authenticity and sincerity into
your physical (and digital) spaces – proving to your
employees that you're serious and that you care about
the Story that you are preaching.

T = Tools and Technology that are utilised within
your business need to further streamline the Story.
Tools and tech should be empowering your staff,

enabling them to achieve your values and goals and allowing them to contribute with 100 percent confidence. Examples include gamification platforms, collaboration tools like slack.com, and any upgraded tech tool that allows seamless implementation of the Story.

S = The (Perfect) Staff Member is the Serena Williams of your business. In real life, we all have heroes we try to emulate, look up to or borrow certain characteristics from. In the workplace, we need the same thing: who is the hero we admire and how defined are his or her actions? More importantly, how can employees mimic this role model?

Ideally, you need a real person in your business who can be a perfect representative or poster image of how to live the Story. But if you don't have somebody like that, you could create fictitious characters or find employees who are living up to these values in one way or another and build a composite perfect staff member. Show them off or highlight them so that your people can have a benchmark to work towards.

Having a role model also helps managers promote and demote staff, because they have a healthier idea of what they are striving for as far as the values are concerned.

Implementing Culture S.T.A.R.S.

Creating a great company culture is often easier said than done, and I would always recommend starting with a Trenovate workshop that aims to unpack the future of the Four Pillars: where your technology, industry, consumers and employees are going. You can't build a culture or strategy around how amazing your business needs to be or how you will sustain it if you can't figure out what your company is going to be like in the next five to ten years.

It's imperative that companies have at least one Chief Future Officer (CFO). The role of the Chief Executive Officer (CEO) is in fact moving towards becoming more of a CFO role, which demands constantly tuning into trends in the Four Pillars, possible disruptors, the changing need states (depending on the market) and the future of employees. By having a finger on the pulse of their ecosystem, brands have the ability to communicate with consumers in a jab-jab-jab-right-hook format: being relevant and adding value without always asking for a sale.

S.T.A.R.S. allows us to focus on our future and to understand what kind of employees we need to hire for the right company ecosystem. This culture must be sustained through constant employee recognition, empowerment and autonomy by using gamification and similar reward-based tactics. In turn, management will move away from *enforcing* the culture to coaching staff on how to *live* the culture. Remember that your employees are consumers and they can be your greatest advocates if there's enough value in it for them. If they operate in an autonomous, creative and free ecosystem, they will also be in a better position to help future consumers by fulfilling a need before asking them to buy something. A business that is focused on being more convenient and personable can create a pull strategy for sales by giving consumers what they desire.

We can't fall into the trap of underestimating the power of adding value and recognition in a world where things that used to cost money are now becoming free. To stay afloat in this changing macrocosm, our business models must continue to adjust internally and externally.

In a nutshell, Culture S.T.A.R.S. facilitates the implementation of an organisational culture that is prepared for your future industry, employee and consumer.

R.A.P.I.D. Innovation

Following Culture S.T.A.R.S., the second part of Step 2 in the Forever Profitable process is R.A.P.I.D. Innovation. Designed to work in tandem, the former is applied with the purpose of *internal*, employee-focused innovation, and the latter for *external*, consumer-focused innovation that also affects your culture and business model.

While Culture S.T.A.R.S. can help you create an agile and future-focused internal culture, when you consider fluctuating consumer needs and industry shifts or disruptions your current business model may look nothing like the one of the future. It needs to be fluid enough to change quickly and adjust to exponentially changing needs.

Robin Sharma sums up the approach eloquently: 'Clarity before mastery.'

By applying R.A.P.I.D. Innovation to your business, you will ask the right questions to gain the *clarity* you need to adopt and implement a business model of the future with *mastery*.

What does it mean to innovate with purpose?
Before we get into the details of R.A.P.I.D. Innovation, let's take a quick look at the word 'innovation' –

one that has, in my opinion, been bastardised and devalued in recent times. Those using it often seem to think that slight business tweaks infer massive innovations – but that is hardly the case.

Not too long ago I saw an advert by 'the most innovative property group in South Africa'. Being in the world of innovation and trends, I was intrigued by their claim, so I looked them up – and I found that their sole substantiation for this bold line was that they opened property show houses on Wednesday afternoons (as opposed to the usual Sunday norm).

For me, that wasn't purposeful innovation. Purposeful innovation requires us to understand real changes in the marketplace, in industries and in technology. It demands that we decipher real changes in our consumers and offer real changes to our employees. We must then merge the trends and insights we find and implement plans that genuinely impact on people and dramatically affect their lives. A show house on a Wednesday afternoon is not going to change my life in any way – it's just being different for the sake of it.

This half-baked approach can be dangerous for organisations, because it can take their focus off the real purpose of innovation and fool them into spending money on gimmicks that don't add value.

A shotgun approach to innovation is likely to yield messy, underwhelming results. Take your time and apply the long game, because a panicked or rushed approach may just muddy your business waters.

R.A.P.I.D. is an acronym that represents the following steps:

R = Rethink your sector. You need to be brave enough to ask new questions about your business, and you need to be willing to jump sectors if necessary in order to stay relevant. To rethink your industry, you need to ask new questions about what your business should be doing. What sector could you be playing in? How can technology enhance what you are doing?

> **Switching examples:** All around us, we find brands that have jumped into other industries in order to stay relevant: Nike became a digital business; Apple became a music business; major US bank Capital One launched coffee shops and yoga studios to build trust with a younger clientele; US toilet paper brand Charmin became a tech-focused public toilet-location service company to stand out from the crowd; FNB became South Africa's largest Apple and Samsung products distribution company. The list goes on.

A = Awareness of your future consumer. This must be brought into the decision-making room when conceptualising innovation. Do you understand your consumers' need states, their value systems and the sectors they engage with? Are you creating innovation based on the future rather than the current needs of the consumer? What does your future consumer look like? Here you can consider the needs I have described in order to uncover how the future consumer's needs differ from the past consumer's needs. (See from p128.)

P = Prototype. Introduce new prototypes across your consumer's journey: the product itself, the packaging it comes in, the service and environment in which it is sold, the technology you use, the social and environmental impact. How are you prototyping and innovating along the customer journey to align with the future consumer's needs?

I = Iterate. In a line attributed to Reed Hoffman, the founder of LinkedIn, 'If you are not embarrassed by the time you launch the first version of your business, you have waited too long.' In other words: come up with a new and innovative version of whatever you're selling and launch it into the market as quickly as possible – *then* experiment, and do it again.

D = Develop. And keep moving. The marketplace is not waiting for you, so don't wait for perfection. Keep iterating and experimenting. Keep launching, refining, developing and doing to see what works. Today's market moves too fast for hesitation and if you don't take some leaps you will find yourself left behind.

STEP 3
Implementing gamification

The third and final step towards being Forever Profitable is all about gamification. From a young age, we create games for ourselves; games that can turn an ordinary activity into something fun and rewarding. This concept of creating and playing games in everyday life can also be applied to enhance routine daily choices or tasks in the workplace. It is an approach that taps into our new-age need for instant gratification and recognition, and it allows companies to effectively alleviate stress in pressure-filled work environments and successfully change consumer and employee behaviours.

In my own experience, I have repeatedly seen that even when working with the most senior company members to craft powerful strategic plans, successfully implementing them can still fall short. In my interaction with other strategists and consultants, the conclusion is invariably the same: the actual adoption and practice of strategies throughout the organisation often leaves much to be desired. As a result, I started looking more closely at this pattern and examined the trends that were being used to address this flaw: I realised that the number one way we can change people's behaviour is through gamification.

Gamification for both consumers *and* employees is necessary so that they feel like they are being incrementally rewarded and recognised as they change their behaviour.

Changing our own behaviour is relatively hard, let alone changing the behaviour of an entire group, so the Three Rs of changing habits mentioned in Chapter 3 come into play here: the Reminder, Routine and Reward concept can be effectively applied via a gamification platform.

Consumer behaviour

As far as the consumer is concerned, there are many ways in which our behaviour is gamified. Businesses have, in fact, been doing this for decades – just think air miles. Since American Airlines introduced their air miles programme in the 1960s, many of us will have tried our best to earn air miles with our most convenient airline. It's a game: the more you fly with this airline, the more free flights you get.

The Discovery example: In South Africa, Discovery applied the concept of air miles to the health-insurance industry, launching Discovery Vitality in 1997, a 'scientifically proven wellness programme' that encourages customers to earn points by making (and recording) healthy lifestyle choices. Today customers are rewarded with tiered discounts at major retailers for exercising, having routine medical checks-ups, buying the right foods and demonstrating other behaviours considered beneficial to health. The company has applied a similar ratings programme to the way it insures cars, encouraging its customers to be better drivers, and it incorporates life assurance and investment into its overall loyalty programme.

Over a period that has seen numerous medical-aid companies fail, Discovery has built itself into the largest (open) medical-aid company in South Africa by a considerable distance – but in my mind they are a gamification platform that just happens to sell insurance.

Discovery Miles, eBucks, ABSA Rewards, airline miles, coffee-shop loyalty points – these are all currencies in consumer-focused games we happily play, because there is something in it for us.

As consumers, gamification gives us constant reward and recognition when our actions are transparent for the whole organisation to see. When this happens, we start acting in a very different way and we change our behaviour to be more in line with the organisational strategy. If we don't like it and we are not playing the game, we leave or we lose out.

For example, if you're not into fitness and you're not reaching your goals on a daily, weekly and annual basis, the Discovery Vitality programme is probably not for you. Personally, I believe that I benefit hugely from health gamification. I live on the sixth floor of my apartment block and if I haven't burned my required daily calories by the time I get home at the end of the day – which I know by looking at my watch – I take the stairs. I enjoy playing games, I like being recognised for my efforts and I really like the large discount I get on my flights and Uber rides. Discovery's gamification has changed the way I behave. And the bonus? I'm healthier for it.

Employee behaviour

Businesses have long played rudimentary 'games' with staff, but nominal rewards like winning employee of the month or receiving a CEO shout-out in a group email or company meeting have lost their lustre in an age when people expect real, measurable incentives. And while annual bonuses and employee prizes will always serve a motivational purpose, the new approach to gamification refines this concept to a daily and weekly level that applies to any staff member at any time, no matter his track record.

When employees are **continuously measured and rewarded** they act differently with more consistency, and **change their behaviour** to be more in line with the organisational strategy.

And if they don't like it and are not playing the game, then – like the customer who's part of a loyalty programme that's not working for him – they simply leave or lose out.

The importance of finding employees who fit your company culture becomes particularly evident here. People tend not to find anything sinister about 'being watched' if the process is transparent and they believe in the end product/result. Those employees you do lose on the implementation of a new gamification rewards programme are likely to be those who were less comfortable with your company culture to begin.

I believe so strongly in the importance of applying a programme of ongoing reward and recognition to employees that, along with a team of talented developers and UX designers, I have created my own dedicated platform called Airbrn. The intention is to help businesses and organisations change their employees' behaviour based on e-learning, and then gamifying the results of that e-learning.

When performance benchmarks such as reaching sales targets are met, employees receive incremental, real recognition and rewards. Whether it's a cash incentive, a weekend away or a day off work, there is a more tangible sense of achievement, which inevitably leads to increased buy-in and productivity.

Ultimately, employees get to a point where they aren't only earning a salary; they're getting daily, weekly and monthly appraisals and have the ability to earn rewards and prizes for acting the way the company wants them to act. It's about tailoring focus, inspiring actions and helping staff to be recognised for their efforts and commitment.

WHERE TO NOW?

Now that we've looked at how to Trenovate in Four Pillars, how to implement Culture S.T.A.R.S. and R.A.P.I.D. Innovation, and how to gamify processes to change behaviour, we have the opportunity to take a multidimensional, holistic approach to the future.

Exploring the Four Pillars of Forever Profitable empowers decision-makers and employees to up-skill and gain knowledge in bite-sized portions. If you run a business, you can set up a series of workshops, each of which should be focused on one pillar at a time, allowing you and your team to investigate and understand the needs in isolation before putting together the bigger picture.

As you start hosting these workshops, your employees, management, executive committee and board members alike will begin to gain the courage to change.

And this is the crux of Forever Profitable: no matter how small or large your business, you need to find the courage to stop relying on what may have worked in the past and look towards a new world in which you can anticipate being taken out of your comfort zone.

The difference between companies that are Forever Profitable and those that aren't is courage.

Everything that's gone into this chapter has been gathered over the last decade, but the Forever Profitable methodology will itself keep evolving as the world evolves. In the meantime, I will continue to apply it to the companies I work with and encourage you to make use of it in your own business.

Now the question remains: what's your Moonshot?

CHAPTER FIVE

CREATING YOUR MOONSHOT

Putting it all together – with an end-goal to change the world!

On the 25th of May 1961, President John F Kennedy addressed US Congress, telling them he believed America should 'commit itself to achieving the goal, before this decade is out, of landing a man on the Moon and returning him safely to the Earth'. In September the following year, he followed it up with a speech in Houston, Texas, in which he justified this massive undertaking, saying:

> We choose to go to the Moon in this decade and do the other things, not because they are easy, but because they are hard; because that goal will serve to organise and measure the best of our energies and skills, because that challenge is one that we are willing to accept, one we are unwilling to postpone, and one we intend to win.

These addresses marked a critical time in modern US and global history, with the latter speech taking its place as one of the great inspirational moments of our age, and Kennedy's vision for his country's future becoming known as the 'Moonshot'.

In May 1961, when Kennedy first revealed his plan, most of the engineering and technology, and even some of the metal alloys that the spaceships would require to withstand the intense heat of space travel, had not yet been invented. The original Moonshot vision was a bold and potentially dangerous mission, but there was little doubt in the collective victor mindset of Americans that it could be achieved.

The Moonshot created an opportunity for people to work together for a Massive Transformative Purpose – a major, aspirational motive driven by a deep desire to achieve a life-changing goal.

With this powerful purpose in place, you could argue that anything is possible. Bud Tribble, vice-president of software technology at Apple (and member of the team that designed the original Apple Macintosh), used the term 'reality distortion field' – apparently extracted from an episode of *Star Trek* – to describe the approach that Steve Jobs took when initiating Moonshot ideas: making people believe that the seemingly impossible is possible. A reality distortion field creates a space in which the confines of known reality and logic are altered by a strong intention and desire to achieve a Moonshot, enabling collaborators to overlook the obstructive technical difficulties involved and create an environment in which their ultimate ambitions can be fulfilled.

In a way, Moonshots can be inspired by the threat of being disrupted. Kennedy himself observed that 'the exploration of space will go ahead, whether we join in it or not'. On a political level, the US was at risk of being disrupted in the 'race for space', having fallen behind to their Cold War nemesis, the Soviet Union, who had been the first to put a satellite (1957) and man (1961) into space. Their competitors were other nations who were rapidly innovating and advancing in science and technology. At the time, you had to be the first or be the follower – it was a measurement of skills and capability.

'Change is the law of life,' Kennedy said. 'And those who look only to the past or present are certain to miss the future.'

Today, conceiving and actualising a Moonshot has never been easier.

Technology is evolving at exponential rates, becoming ever cheaper and more accessible; we have the ability to collaborate with great minds around the world at almost no cost (whether directly or indirectly); we are less afraid or inhibited to dream big; and we see more and more examples of Moonshot thinking affecting our lives to inspire us in turn.

As individuals and companies, we just need to decide which side of history we want to be on: the side that creates these massive transformative businesses and movements, or the side that thinks we're just in a faster-paced version of 1990.

A serial groundbreaker like Elon Musk – of SpaceX, Tesla and PayPal fame – 'suffers' from being in a reality distortion field, and all over the world I see so many people similarly afflicted by this happy malady. No matter what anybody says or thinks, when you have a Massive Transformative Purpose – even when you can't really describe it to the last detail – and you understand the core of what you want to do, you will follow your highest excitement and pursue it with enthusiasm.

Moonshots take you out of your comfort zone and place you firmly on the trajectory to your best possible future – one in which you can reach your goals and aspirations.

We already have so many tools with which to innovate on a grand scale, and it's only going to get easier, so I urge you to dream big, create Moonshots and see how the world will interact with you and react to you. People want to be around those who are passionate and are shaping the future. You'll always have those who naysay – the haters – and those who warn you that you're acting too big for your boots. In the words of Peter Diamandis, 'People will resist breakthrough ideas until the moment they're accepted as the new norm.'

There is a great talk by American author and speaker Brené Brown, in which she explains how she became extremely insecure after her first video went viral and she was exposed to the resulting comments on YouTube, including many from cynics and trolls calling her fat, stupid and ridiculous. The response sank her into a depression. It took her months to snap out of it and realise that if people are not operating in the same arena as her, their criticisms don't stick and don't count. Creating, believing in and driving a Moonshot compels you to think like a victor, not a victim. It relies on your ability to be charismatic towards your followers and irreverent towards the doubters. If you can apply the art of irreverence and glide past the trepidation, you can be victorious.

SUCCESSFUL MOONSHOTS

Any new technology or innovation that has radically shifted our lives started off as a Moonshot.

Henry Ford had a Moonshot when he conceptualised a production line that would allow him to build cars for the masses – and he turned it into a reality. Thomas Edison's most important Moonshot (arguably) was his desire to make cheap electric lighting widely available – which he did by inventing a practical, commercially viable light bulb. The mobile phone revolution was a Moonshot that changed the way we were able to communicate, and now we all carry a phone (and the internet) in our pockets. The fact that so many of us have personal computers at home is the result of Bill Gates introducing his Windows Moonshot.

For more recent examples, we can look to Elon Musk (born in Pretoria) as a Moonshot ambassador and an expert at generating transformative ideas, be it in online banking (PayPal), electric cars and battery packs (Tesla) or, literally, in Moonshots (SpaceX). Google X is also a Moonshot powerhouse that operates as a subsidiary organisation of the conglomerate, incubating the research and development of massive transformative purposes. Driverless cars, delivery drones and smart contact lenses are just a few examples of what Google X has brewing in its pots.

In South Africa Raymond Ackerman accomplished his Moonshot by revolutionising the way we shopped, expanding the Pick n Pay supermarket chain from almost nothing in 1967 to a subcontinental powerhouse that employs 50,000 people today. And more recently, local food delivery service and startup OrderIn is a good example of a company that has achieved a Moonshot, by changing the way we order food, both at home and at work.

More Moonshot examples: Today, a private company sends rockets to the International Space Station: SpaceX has a staff of around 5,000 compared to the Apollo's project's 400,000, and it's now aiming to send a manned rocket to the moon – a literal Moonshot – in 2018.

A private individual is driving the eradication of one of the world's deadliest diseases: Bill Gates has helped reduce deaths from malaria by 60 percent since 2000.

A student invented a communications platform used by a quarter of the world's population: Mark Zuckerberg launched Facebook in 2004 while still a teenager; it had 1.86 billion active users by the end of 2016.

In short: world-changing opportunities – be they business plans, social movements or cultural shifts – are becoming available to anyone with internet access and the right mindset.

Anybody who has created a new way of interacting, connecting, buying, developing products and tech or delivering services has achieved a Moonshot and has changed the world around us in their own way. Regardless of the industry these innovations have positively affected, these Moonshots will have been driven by a vision that went beyond making a profit. The idea of becoming a new type of billionaire means creating something as drastic, large and poignant as these examples.

I'm not saying we must all aim to invent the world's first teleportation device – though that would be nice – but Moonshots *should* be grandiose and monumental in one way or another.

WHERE DO YOU START?

Though I am encouraging you to think big, the first step of your Moonshot should simply be about getting your idea off the ground. Taking the leap into global markets is, as we've seen, much easier than ever before, and this is where you can let your imagination fly. But I would venture to say that many Moonshots start off – or, at least, appear to start off – with unassuming and achievable goals.

Popular seafood chain Ocean Basket is a good South African example. What started out as a small, amiable Mediterranean deli in Pretoria in 1995 has expanded into a multinational franchise with more than two hundred restaurants in sixteen countries. Did founder Fats Lazarides know back then that his vision of serving affordable seafood would take off as it has? Perhaps not, but his Moonshot of serving good and affordable seafood to South Africans was clear and delivered with passion.

Then again, that was more than two decades ago, when dial-up internet had barely made it to our shores.

Today, the world is not local any more; it's global. Despite cultural and sociological differences, the people of our global village often share the same needs, problems and desires – and you now have the power to positively affect so many lives across the planet with the mere swipe of a finger. For you to think locally is thus to limit your potential and to do an injustice to yourself and the world around you.

By applying your mind, your skills and your knowledge to a Moonshot idea you will be looking to develop a solution that has the power to change many people's lives – an idea that may have positively affected a hundred people in the past could now affect a hundred thousand; one that affected a thousand before could affect several million or more today.

It's important to think big – to think exponential, not linear. You have to forcibly overcome the natural human inclination to focus on your immediate surrounds, the area that you live and operate in, your own small business. The reality is that 'your area' is now the entire planet, and the solutions you create with your immediate environment in mind may also be relevant in very different communities or areas all around the world.

Starting locally in the environment you understand well still makes sense, but the intention of **scaling your Moonshot globally should be the inevitable goal.**

You need a Moonshot idea that will leave you with no other choice but to dream courageously and be brave enough to believe that you can have an impact on a global scale.

At this point, it's easy – perhaps even natural – to feel discouraged or to start inviting victim thoughts into your mind. 'I could never change the world... I could never operate on such a vast scale... I could never be an Elon Musk.' Go back and read chapters 2 and 3! And then get cracking...

Of course, you must start somewhere, and inevitably you will always end up catering to one of the world's major markets: the mature awareness, emerging awareness or less-affluent markets. Remember, you may cater to one of these markets in your town or city, but these markets are found all over the world.

The South African examples:

Elim, a South African spa-product company based in Melkbosstrand, is a great example of a brand that solved a local problem that happened to be a global problem. Its CEO Shantelle Booysen saw a gap in the local pedicure and manicure markets and started developing and producing a range of targeted spa products in 2004. It wasn't long before she realised that the shortage of products focusing on hands and feet wasn't just South African; it was universal. Today, Elim products are exported around the world.

Bio-Oil, which was formulated in South Africa in 1987 by German chemist Dieter Beier, is another local-to-international Moonshot success story – though the success was not immediate. In 2000, brothers David and Justin Letscher saw the potential of the product, and acquired it from Beier. Though it had had little market impact to that point, it was extremely effective at treating scars and stretch marks. Identifying the absence of similar products, the Letschers focused on this in particular, changing the packaging to better reflect it and effectively using customer testimonials in their marketing campaigns. Bio-Oil quickly gained global traction, becoming a multimillion-dollar business and 'the No.1 selling scar and stretch mark product in 24 countries since its global launch in 2002'.

Though the ultimate intention should always be global, sometimes a locally or regionally executed Moonshot is necessary, especially if you need a testing ground before you can make the giant leap.

The African examples: Silicon Valley startup Zipline is one of several companies to have pioneered delivery of supplies to remote areas that can't be accessed via reliable infrastructure. Whereas federal drone legislations in the US are still in the making, and are thus an inhibiting factor for drone operators, Zipline has been instrumental in formalising drone regulations in Rwanda in central Africa. The mountainous country suffers heavy seasonal rains that can render roads unusable, so it makes an ideal proving ground for Zipline to deliver blood, plasma and other medical supplies by catapault-launched drone. Now rural hospitals and clinics can place their orders via text message, and the deliveries are parachuted to them in a matter of minutes, rather than hours, at the same cost as before. This is a Moonshot shared by others, with companies like Matternet making similar strides in Malawi where it delivers HIV test kits. Once proved at regional level, it's a matter of time before drone deliveries become a globally feasible solution.

FINDING YOUR MOONSHOT IDEA

Now to the crux of it all: coming up with your Moonshot plan.

To find your Moonshot, you need to channel your natural inclinations or talents into a vehicle that you will remain committed to, come what may. It's critical that you identify these talents and then stick to them no matter what.

Combining inherent skill and personal experience, preferably in your field of expertise, will allow you to solve a tangible problem with real passion. But achieving your Moonshot must come naturally to you.

What excites you? How can you apply your aptitude to solving a problem that you are familiar with? Your Moonshot should start by focusing on a real scenario that you or the people around you are experiencing – and if it's globally applicable, even better. Then you need to ask yourself if it fits into your natural inclinations and passions.

The personal examples: You may have thought, at some point in the course of this book, What's *your* Moonshot, Mr Author? Well, I have two of them.

I love my work, and from it I've worked out that my real passion is to change the questions that South Africans ask about South Africa. I have been able to create a Moonshot called 'RISE of the Nation', a speaker platform that aims to attract top speakers from around the world to South Africa. The concept came about because I choose to live as an optimist – some of my friends might describe me as a militant optimist – and have become somewhat allergic to people who focus their energy on the negative. (You may have noticed that I have a thing about victim mindsets.)

With this disposition, I attended a business breakfast seminar called State of the Nation (no, not the presidential address) in 2015. I was looking forward to hearing some of South Africa's top speakers unpack the national situation and reveal the opportunities in our country, but about halfway through I realised that the event was not so much about the *state* of our nation, but more about the *negatives* of our nation. It appealed directly to the victim mindset – inviting it to come right out and play in the mud. I felt irritated and depressed. After muscling through a painstaking three-quarters of the event, I got up and left.

Not only was I feeling angry, frustrated and negative about my country, I was also disappointed that the organisers had missed an incredible opportunity to inspire over a thousand corporate decision-makers to look for amazing opportunities locally; to do good and make profit – for themselves and others. Why had they chosen to take the low road?

Maybe if I hadn't stopped myself from peeing in my nappy, I would have stayed to relish the negative prospects. I might have gone to the pub with some delegates afterwards, complained over a glass of whisky and forgotten about my elusive mistress: possibility. Instead, I *chose* to be an optimist.

Within hours of leaving the event, my victor hat firmly on head, I started formulating my Moonshot. I saw the situation as an opportunity and was inspired to set up my own platform, RISE of the Nation. At the time of going to print with this book, we have secured a partnership with Media24 for national media coverage and are in discussion with formidable international speakers such as Simon Sinek and Sir Ken Robinson, as well as top local speakers to talk to corporates with a clear brief: to touch on our challenges, but focus on the opportunities for us to *rise* and bring about massive change to our country. Effectively to adopt a Forever Profitable approach. Our inaugural event was an unforgettable presentation in late 2016 by legendary US journalist and *New York Times* bestselling author Cal Fussman. The Moonshot had begun... (It went down so well that I asked Cal to write the foreword to this book.)

The goal is to get the speakers out here so that they can share their knowledge and help us ask better questions about our country. **This is a Moonshot because it is a problem I am passionate about and have access to and is one I believe I can help solve.** My natural inclination towards connecting people or brands and bringing people together means that I have the right skills to make my Moonshot work.

A second Moonshot of mine is Airbrn, the gamification platform mentioned on p182. It's aimed at changing the culture of organisations around the world by applying my Culture S.T.A.R.S. method to implement fundamental shifts in internal culture. Again, as an experienced strategist, I have a natural inclination towards future-proofing organisations and facilitating change – it's a real problem that I am actually seeing and am dedicated to solving.

Following this active advice, I must add a word of warning. If your Moonshot is targeted at solving a problem that is beyond your knowledge and skills, you may be setting yourself up for a pointless ride. For instance, I know that we are using too much fossil-fuel energy, I would love to be able to do something about it, and the answer to this great issue of our time has Moonshot written all over it. But my personal talents do not lie in the field of reusable energy and I know little about harnessing solar, wind or any other natural power. This is not a problem that mixes well with who I am and what I am good at.

IMPLEMENTING YOUR MOONSHOT

The end goal of a Moonshot is usually a great achievement that will require a fair amount of implementation along the way, but this mustn't scare you out of your processes or obscure your vision of getting there. Since your timeline will most likely be an estimate, you will always be focusing on the next step rather than the end goal.

Right now the next step in my RISE of the Nation Moonshot is to reach out to the people we want to attract to South Africa for the speaker events we will be hosting. When I first started actively planning this Moonshot – which was how I always thought of it in my mind – I discovered that the price for top personalities was far above our budget. The solution was to find organisations that would be interested in partnering with us. With this goal in mind, I happened to come across someone who works at Media24 and we were able to enter a partnership with one of Africa's most important and influential media companies, giving us exposure to millions of South Africans.

In this instance, the key was to have that vision so that when opportunity knocks you can welcome it in.

The implementation of the Moonshot may very well happen in increments and the individual steps can become secondary to pursuing the inevitable end goal. Having all the answers or knowing where the funding will come from are, in fact, things that can hamper your progress. If you just move towards the vision slowly and strategically, implementation will work itself out in an organic, intelligent way.

When John F Kennedy delivered his original Moonshot speech, I don't think he knew exactly how it was going to happen – he couldn't have, because no-one did! Yes, he was aware of the hurdles, but because he created hype and hope he was able to attract people who shared his vision; he created his own reality distortion field.

Even though Kennedy would not live to witness the monumental occasion in human history when *Apollo 11* landed on the Moon in the Sea of Tranquillity on the 20th of July 1969, and astronaut Neil Armstrong took his giant leap onto the lunar surface, it had been his vision and his words that fuelled the process.

Developing your Moonshot concept is a process that can take a few hours or several years. Based on my own approach, I have created an easy-to-follow roadmap to guide you in making your Moonshot happen.

STEP 1: REALIGN SELF-PERCEPTION

Are you a victim or a victor? Get real about whether you are approaching the world and your future with a victim or victor mindset. Listen to your internal dialogue: are you being kind to yourself and are you prioritising your emotions?

Stop peeing in your nappy. Train your brain to get out of its comfort-zone routine and replace victim traits with victor mindset habits.

Remind yourself to be audacious. This might mean stepping out of your comfort zone and finding the courage to try something that seems impossible. If there's anything you can learn from failure, it's not to be afraid of it. Moonshots rely on a brazen, unhindered approach.

Treat everyone as an equal opportunity and practise the art of irreverence. The sooner you realise that you can't make everyone happy, the sooner you can invite like-minded people into your tribe; people who bring out the best in you and support your Moonshot.

Act with interiority. Does your inside reflect what you project on the outside? Approach opportunities with equanimity and don't subscribe to drama.

STEP 2: EVALUATE & INNOVATE

Tune into the frequency of opportunities at all times.

Use this mindset to evaluate every scenario and problem you encounter to find a potential solution (and a potential Moonshot). You can start by analysing important trends in your field of interest.

Know your Four Pillars. Does your Moonshot lie in disrupting an industry – perhaps your own? Dissect the relevant consumer and employee needs, your market, the future of your industry, the future of technology and the applicable trends. If necessary, employ a trend specialist to help you do so – an objective approach is key here.

Where there is a consumer challenge, there is a potential solution. Looking for your own challenges as a consumer is a good place to start. (For me, RISE of the Nation was the solution to my personal dislike of doom mongering.)

Use your natural abilities to innovate with purpose and look for inspiration from global and local entrepreneurs. Move forward by following the R.A.P.I.D. Innovation process:

Re-think your sector
Be **Aware**
Prototype
Iterate and experiment
Develop and **Do**

If in doubt, consult with a strategist to help you build your roadmap with R.A.P.I.D. Innovation in mind. Again, objectivity is key.

STEP 3: PLAN & IMPLEMENT

Share your vision. For your Moonshot to start gaining momentum, it's imperative to share your vision with like-minded talent and build a team of people who are experts in their field and can do things that you can't.

As an example, for my Airbrn gamification platform Moonshot I've built a small but powerful team consisting of:

A developer – because that's not my area of expertise;
A user experience designer – also a specialist role;
An operations and accounting man – to make sure the 'i's are dotted and 't's are crossed;

An account director – for sales and client relations;
An idea generator, driver, strategic salesperson and 'Moonshot Guy' – that's me!

In this case, each of us owns a percentage of the concept (and business), which helped to get everyone on board. However you achieve it, you have to gather your tribe and start to build the company based on the Moonshot goal. The right people will be excited to join your crusade and deliver your Moonshot to the world. Remain persistent.

Launch locally. And remember: do it sooner rather than later – because if you're not embarrassed by your first launch, you've waited to long. Your primary objective of launching is to gain traction, then iterate.

Implement gamification. Reinforce value and innovation strategies by rewarding consumer and employee behaviour using gamification tactics.

Plant seeds. As soon as you have your Moonshot idea, start connecting with people globally to find out who's looking for a similar solution. Don't underestimate the possibility of expanding globally – at the time of writing this, we have launched our gamification platform locally, it is being beta tested in four companies, and we have two agents in Brazil and New Zealand waiting to start testing. All of this has happened after only eighteen months of building the platform and team.

Play the long game. Don't force fast results that will cause stress. Be patient.

STEP 4: MOONSHOT!

Your Moonshot might not go as you planned. It could happen gradually or suddenly.

When your Moonshot is successful, don't stop innovating. Keep levelling up and graduating to your next Moonshot.

WHAT'S YOUR MOONSHOT?

A Moonshot can be any ambitious or pioneering project; a game-changing idea that is driven by curiosity and determination, rather than a natural progression that might satisfy a feasibility study. Such ideas may sound magical, mythical or seemingly impossible, but they have never been more achievable. Now it's up to you to find yours – you have the tools and you know how to apply them.

To begin, seek clarity – in your own thinking and in your understanding of your consumers' behaviour. Because from clarity comes mastery. And with mastery you can think big to drive change and shape the future.

When you commit to your vision, remember that like-minded people won't criticise you; they will encourage and constructively help you. Don't engage with the pessimists who aren't in the same arena as you. You *must* think big. You *must* dare to dream. It may sound presumptive, but the world needs as many positive Moonshots as it can get. So start planning yours now, not just for yourself, but because humanity needs us to follow our highest excitement and create dreams to become the new breed of billionaire: people who impact billions of people's lives positively.

Now, go and master your Moonshot!

NOTES & RESOURCES

The information in *What's Your Moonshot?*, and in particular my Forever Profitable methodology described in these pages, has largely been inspired by the many clients, peers and teachers I've interacted with over the years. I have absorbed, adapted, borrowed and refashioned their work in an ongoing process of continuous research, from face-to-face interactions to hearing them talk in person and online to reading company reports, blogs, articles, websites and more. For this I am grateful (and I hope I have, at times, assisted them). I refer to only a fraction of these people in the chapter notes below and then provide a selected bibliography of the books and websites that have most influenced my thinking and the material in the book. To the many I've no doubt forgotten to mention, I sincerely apologise.

CHAPTER 1: AGHA-JOON

p28... Peeing in your nappy: This concept comes from the idea that short-term pain yields long-term gain, encapsulated for me by a fascinating study on children in the US in the 1960s and 1970s. Known as the 'Stanford marshmallow experiment', it involved sitting each child in a room individually, giving them a single marshmallow and telling them they were going to be left alone in the room with the marshmallow for 15 minutes. If they didn't eat the marshmallow in that time, they would be rewarded with another one; but if they did eat the marshmallow, they wouldn't get another. Naturally, some children ate the marshmallow and others didn't. Years later, follow-up studies revealed that the kids who were able to endure the delayed gratification of waiting for the adult to return and then receiving a second marshmallow had demonstrated better overall success in life, scoring measurably higher on intelligence and competence tests. The kids who had eaten their marshmallow and couldn't wait for their 'reward' were effectively peeing in their nappies for short-term gain without thinking about the long-term consequences.

p34... The long game: The five-day game versus one-day game comparison originated from my observations of a very good friend, Paul. A passionate national team supporter, Paul travels across South Africa to watch as many games as possible. I can visibly see his mood change when he is attending five-day games, compared to when he is watching a one-day game. For the latter, his mood is frantic and mildly delirious; it reminds me of a company's disposition when making imprudent business decisions.

p38... There was a time when I practised Kundalini yoga at a studio in Cape Town, where the Yogi Bhajan quote appeared prominently on one of the walls. I identified with Kundalini yoga and its philosophies of awakening the teacher within and finding the guru inside yourself. It's very much in line with the idea that 'you master what you teach' and that, if you invoke the guru within, you become a teacher. All of us have something of the teacher inside of us.

CHAPTER 2: VICTIM?

p42... Victim and victor: Although I have formulated my own interpretation of the victim and victor traits in these pages, it was Seth Godin's *Purple Cow* that originally instilled this thinking in me in 2008. He used the metaphor of creating a purple cow – instead of a brown, black or white one – as a way of articulating that we need to stop being followers: there are enough average cows out there. It helped me understand the concept of looking for opportunities rather than challenges or problems.

p42... Internal dialogue: I was asked to put together a talk for *Creative Mornings*, a breakfast talk that is hosted around the world (see creativemornings.com). The theme was 'Language' and I started thinking about how language affects our daily lives, which led me to question where language comes from and the way we choose to speak (and listen) based on our own internal dialogue. I became increasingly interested in 'voices' and 'messages' that are not visible or audible to us, but which we are still receptive to and which influence us more than we like to know. Internal dialogue is reflected in facial expressions, body language and tonality. I named the talk 'Language as a superpower' because I believe that speaking and harnessing unseen and unheard language is a masterful ability. Although much of the thoughts around internal dialogue came from my own realisation that I was being hard on myself, Richard Carlson's *Don't Sweat The Small Stuff... And It's All Small Stuff* can be considered a solid reference here. Carlson manages to simplify the complexities of holding back on passing judgement or criticism. I find any work around inner dialogue to be easier said than done, but it's ultimately the awareness and continuous reminders that make incremental differences. Eckhart Tolle's *The Power of Now* also guided my thinking around being a witness to the 'voice' and listening to internal dialogue. I must also cite *The Untethered Soul: The journey beyond yourself* by Michael A Singer, which delves into the self-questioning process in which you discover that you are *not* the voice in your mind. Singer argues that the voice is often schizophrenic and erratic and may lead you to believe truths that are yet to transpire. Finally, Tripp Lanier's *The New Man: Beyond the macho jerk and the new age wimp* podcast (www.thenewmanpodcast.com) was also a helpful resource, specifically in relation to the 'modern man'.

CHAPTER 3: VICTOR!

p68... Mindset and habits: Charles Duhigg's *The Power of Habit* deserves buckets of credit for my interpretation of how habits shape mindsets and patterns of behaviour. The thoughts and concepts to do with the habit loop, in particular, must be attributed to Duhigg, but my exploration of habits also led me to discovering James Clear – see his article on 'the 3 Rs': *The 3 Rs of Habit Change: How to start new habits that actually stick* (www.jamesclear.com). Dr Joe Dispenza, a neuroscientist who writes, speaks, consults and teaches, has a more interesting take on the habit loop, explaining that our minds are our personalities and our personalities are our behaviours; our behaviours are our habits and our habits are our rituals. Therefore, in order for you to change your mind, you need to change the ritual that will affect your habits, behaviour, personality and mind. If you're interested in delving deeper into how the habit loop influences so many aspects of our lives, I suggest you look into some of the captivating stories on advertising pioneer Claude C Hopkins, who effectively constructed the reason we brush our teeth every day.

p75... Interiority and equanimity: The TEDx Talk *The Art Of Being Yourself* by Caroline McHugh, available on YouTube, played a large part in solidifying the concepts of interiority and equanimity for me. In this talk McHugh argues that interiority best describes the space between superiority and inferiority. She believes that people with charisma or X-factor or who are thought of as 'larger than life' most likely come from places of interiority and strong spirit.

p78... 'Crisis News Network': This term was taken from Peter Diamandis's podcast *Exponential Wisdom*, which I listen to whenever he releases an episode.

p80... The art of irreverence: My late friend Sean Morgan was the master of irreverence. I loved that he never cared what anybody thought of him. He used to advise me that the opinions of others should flow off you like water off a duck's back. He also taught me to embrace simplicity and work towards a 'R50k Life': he maintained that earning R50,000 every month would allow you to live well yet simply and without the need for or reliance on excess. Another worthy take on the topic, which contributed to my understanding of irreverence, is a book called *The Life-Changing Magic Of Not Giving A Fuck* by Sarah Knight. The extended title says it all: *How to stop spending time you don't have with people you don't like doing things you don't want to do (A no f*cks given guide).* Knight's no-nonsense approach allowed me to differentiate between the things that really mattered and the things I had to let go of in order to move forward with a clear and focused mind. *The Charisma Myth* by Olivia Fox Cabane also encouraged me to take a closer look at the concept of irreverence and the differences between warm/confident irreverence and cold/arrogant irreverence.

CHAPTER 4: FOREVER PROFITABLE

p104... Forever Profitable: The list of those who have influenced my Forever Profitable methodologies is long and worthy, and includes the likes of Jacob Morgan (see his *The Future of Work* podcast at thefutureorganization. com), Robin Sharma (podcasts from www.robinsharma.com), Tim Ferris (see *The Tim Ferris Show* at tim.blog), and Tony Robbins (podcasts from www.tonyrobbins.com).

p107 The changing foundations of capitalism: With regards to my stance on the future of capitalism and its changing foundations of energy, communication and transport, Jeremy Rifkin is my go-to man. Best-selling author of *The Zero Marginal Cost Society*, Rifkin predicted the 'eclipse of capitalism' years ago. His work focuses on the impact of a new economic future and should be interesting to anyone in business today. Find it on YouTube and Google.

p112... Exponential growth: The exponential potential of modern technology was arguably first discovered, or at least elucidated, by Gordon Moore, a Silicon Valley pioneer and co-founder of Fairchild Semiconductor and Intel, who 'described a doubling every year in the number of components per integrated circuit' in the 1960s. Moore's Law, which can be simplified to the notion that computational speeds double on a regular basis – usually given as between eighteen months and three years, depending on the specifics – is named for him. What makes the concept of 'exponential growth' so powerful is that there is this observable evidence of its existence; in other words, it cannot be ignored.

p115... The Six Ds: Peter Diamandis and Steven Kotler must be credited for the reference to 'The Six Ds', as first mentioned in *Bold: How to go big, create wealth and impact the world.* The authors' talks can be found on YouTube and on the Singularity Hub (www.singularityhub.com). Although my interpretation deviates slightly from Diamandis's original Ds, the underlying ideas of exponential growth and change are what make being Forever Profitable so relevant and necessary in the pursuit of your Moonshot. As to the claim that 'There are going to be seven billion people on the internet by 2023', there are varying statistics and forecasts around this figure, but I found Diamandis compelling in its justification, both in *Bold* and in online articles. Cisco, the tech conglomerate, cites the more cautious estimate of 4.1 billion people online by 2020 (www.cisco.com), while websites like www.statista.com claim there were already 3.5 billion online by 2016, which lends credence to the Diamandis prediction.

p128... Need states: These were influenced by a *Future Laboratory* presentation that I attended. See thefuturelaboratory.com.

p150... The future of your employee: There are many differing dates, some of them quite specific, from various sources regarding the timeline classification of Baby Boomers and Generations X, Y and Z. I referred to various online references to assign the general time frames that I think make best sense from our perspective today, including the article *Here is when each generation begins and ends, according to facts* by Philip Bump, originally from *The Wire*, accessed at www.theatlantic.com.

p174... R.A.P.I.D. Innovation: Two examples of companies that were able to rethink their sector are mentioned briefly in this section (on p176): Charmin and Capital One. They have both asked new questions and applied horizontal innovation to move away from their comfort zones and focus on changing consumer needs. Charmin's 'Sit Or Squat' app, which serves as a public toilet locator and rating tool (www.sitorsquat.com), is an example of a creative innovation that is still relevant to the brand's core product: toilet paper. Capital One turned the banking experience into a casual, relaxed environment by transforming key branches into cafés with 'digital lifestyle coaches' in place of bank tellers; they reimagined banking for a new generation of clients with new needs, particularly the need to trust a company in an industry (banking) that has suffered considerable image damage recently. Google provides good information on both brands.

CHAPTER 5: CREATING YOUR MOONSHOT

p188... Moonshots, MTPs and reality distortion fields: The two JFK speeches are sometimes conflated into one – 'the moonshot speech'. For me, his address to Congress, the month after Yuri Gagarin became the first man in space, was JFK's real leap of faith, a direct response to the Soviets' political projections that relied on his belief in American ingenuity and commitment. The more famous 'We choose to go to the moon' address at Rice University in Houston came more than a year later. Both are available on YouTube. Once again Peter Diamandis was inspirational for this chapter, in particular his podcast *Exponential Wisdom* (also featuring Dan Sullivan), which is a great source of information and inspiration. His article *How to disrupt yourself with moonshot thinking and unholy alliances* greatly informs this chapter. It's available on the Singularity Hub (www.singularityhub.com), where I also first came across the term 'Massive Transformational Purpose' or MTP. From there I found the term 'Reality Distortion Field' and discovered that, not only had it been used by Bud Tribble in 1981 to describe Steve Jobs, but it had in fact first been scripted in an episode of *Star Trek* (Season 1, Episode 11/12) as a term, according to Wikipedia, 'used to describe how the aliens created their own new world through mental force' – appropriate to a lot of my work. References to Brené Brown are taken primarily from her website www. brenebrown.com, but also from viewing footage of her speaking events over the past few years. The examples of company Moonshots referenced throughout the chapter are some of those that I have come across in my work, with information gleaned from company websites, news sites and Google.

SELECTED BIBILOGRAPHY

BOOKS

Abundance: The future is better than you think by Peter Diamandis and Steven Kotler (Free Press, 2012)

Bold: How to go big, create wealth and impact the world by Peter Diamandis and Steven Kotler (Simon & Schuster Paperbacks, 2015)

Don't Blame Me! How to stop blaming yourself and other people by Tony Gough (Sheldon Press, 1990)

*Don't Sweat The Small Stuff... And It's All Small Stuff:
Simple ways to keep the little things from overtaking
your life* by Richard Carlson (Hyperion, 1997)

Mindset: How you can fulfil your potential by
Dr Carol S Dweck (Ballantine Books, 2008)

Purple Cow by Seth Godin (Penguin Books, 2003)

*The Charisma Myth: How anyone can master the art and
science of personal magnetism* by Olivia Fox Cabane
(Penguin Group, 2012)

*The How Of Happiness: A practical guide to getting
what you want* by Sonja Lyubomirsky (Piatkus, 2007)

The Life-Changing Magic Of Not Giving A Fuck by Sarah
Knight (Little, Brown & Company, 2015)

*The Power of Habit: Why we do what we do
and how to change* by Charles Duhigg
(William Heinemann, 2012)

The Power of Now by Eckhart Tolle (Namaste Publishing,
1997)

*The Zero Marginal Cost Society: The internet of things,
the collaborative commons, and the eclipse of
capitalism* by Jeremy Rifkin (Palgrave Macmillan, 2014)

The Untethered Soul: The journey beyond yourself by
Michael A Singer (New Harbinger Publications, 2007)

WEBSITES & PODCASTS

atap.google.com

en.wikipedia.org

videos.singularityu.org

www.bizcommunity.com

www.brenebrown.com

www.cisco.com

www.fastcompany.com

www.flyzipline.com

www.foet.org

www.forbes.com

www.fourhourworkweek.com

www.ft.com

www.givingpledge.org

www.huffingtonpost.com

www.independent.co.uk

www.jamesclear.com

www.jfklibrary.org

www.jwtintelligence.com

www.lendingclub.com

www.mawingunetworks.com

www.mttr.net

www.oceanbasket.com

www.opic.gov

www.oxforddictionaries.com

www.pcmag.com

www.quantamagazine.org

www.raconteur.net

www.robinsharma.com

www.singularityhub.com

www.singularityu.org

www.sitorsquat.com

www.slack.com

www.su.org

www.tesla.com

www.theatlantic.com

www.thefinancialbrand.com

www.thefutureorganization.com

www.theguardian.com

www.theverge.com

www.thoughtcatalog.com

www.thyn.com

www.tonyrobbins.com

www.unicef.org

www.venturebeat.com

www.youtube.com

ACKNOWLEDGEMENTS

I would like to acknowledge all my business partners – good and bad, we have taught each other so much.

Thank you to the talented people who helped me put this book together. To be an author has been a dream of mine, and it would never have happened without the very smart people who guided and helped me. In particular, thank you to the wonderful Kirsten Molyneaux.

 john.sanei

IamJohnSanei

johnsanei

johnsanei

www.johnsanei.com

Printed in Poland
by Amazon Fulfillment
Poland Sp. z o.o., Wrocław